BEER:
WHAT TO
DRINK
NEXT

STERLING EPICURE
New York

An Imprint of Sterling Publishing
387 Park Avenue South
New York, NY 10016

Conceived, edited, and designed by
Marshall Editions
The Old Brewery
6 Blundell Street
London N7 9BH

www.marshalleditions.com
First published in Great Britain as *The Beer Select-O-Pedia* in 2014
© 2014 Marshall Editions

Editorial Director Sorrel Wood
Design Rawshock Design
Editor Cathy Meeus
Editorial Assistants Philippa Davis, Lucy Kingett
Photography Simon Pask
Production Nikki Ingram

ISBN 978-1-4549-1006-0

Distributed in Canada by Sterling Publishing
c/o Canadian Manda Group, 165 Dufferin Street
Toronto, Ontario, Canada M6K 3H6

For information about custom editions, special sales, and premium and corporate purchases, please contact
Sterling Special Sales at 800-805-5489 or specialsales@sterlingpublishing.com.

Manufactured in China
2 4 6 8 10 9 7 5 3 1

www.sterlingpublishing.com

BEER: WHAT TO DRINK NEXT

MICHAEL LARSON

STERLING EPICURE
New York

The Beer Select-O-Pedia:
A Periodic Table of Beer Origins

22 **Go** English Golden

24 **Ob** Ordinary Bitter	36 **Ir** Irish Red Ale	44 **Eo** English Old Ale	52 **Bn** English Brown Ale	60 **Ss** Sweet Stout	72 **Wit** Witbier	80 **Spa** Belgian Strong Pale Ale	88 **Tr** Tripel	98 **Bli** Belgian IPA
26 **Bb** Best Bitter	38 **Mac** Scottish Ales	46 **Es** English Strong Old Ale	54 **Ep** English Porter	62 **Os** Oatmeal Stout	74 **Gs** Gose	82 **Ch** Bière de Champagne	90 **Bpa** Belgian Pale Ale	100 **S** Saison
28 **Sb** Strong/Extra Special Bitter	40 **Bar** English Barley Wine	48 **Ww** Winter Warmer	56 **Bp** Baltic Porter	64 **Fs** Foreign/Extra Stout	76 **Be** Berliner Weisse	84 **Kw** Kristalweizen	92 **L** Lambic	102 **Bdg** Bière de Garde
30 **Pa** Pale Ale	42 **We** Strong Scotch Ale	50 **Mi** Dark Mild	58 **Ds** Irish Dry Stout	66 **Ims** Imperial Russian Stout	78 **Kol** Kölsch	86 **Wb** Weissbier	94 **G** Gueuze	104 **Dk** Dunkelweizen
32 **Ipa** India Pale Ale							96 **Lf** Fruit Lambic	106 **Fl** Flanders Red
34 **Lm** Light/Pale Mild								

158 **Aml** American Lager	164 **Ppl** Pre-Prohibition Lager	170 **Gf** Gluten-free	176 **Apa** American Pale Ale	182 **Si** Single Hop IPA	188 **Pu** Pumpkin Ale	194 **Cc** California Common
160 **Pl** Pale Lager	166 **Ab** American Blonde/Golden Ale	172 **Aw** American Style Wheat	178 **Ai** American IPA	184 **Aal** American Amber Lager	190 **Amb** American Amber	196 **Ft** Fruit Beers
162 **Am** American Malt Liquor	168 **Cr** Cream Ale	174 **Ry** Rye Beer	180 **Wh** Wet Hop	186 **Di** Double/Imperial IPA	192 **Wi** American Wild Ale	198 **Usb** American Barley Wine

The periodic table is grouped according to where different styles of beer most famously originate—most types of beer are available from craft brewers the world over. Use the numbers to find out more about each style: turn to that page to discover recommended brewers, tasting notes, and also three beers to try.

142 **Smk** Rauchbier			
108 **Alt** Altbier	126 **Gp** German Pilsner	132 **De** Dortmunder Export	144 **Tb** Traditional Bock
110 **Rg** Roggenbier	128 **Bop** Bohemian Pilsner	134 **Mk** Maibock	146 **Md** Munich Dunkel
112 **Du** Dubbel	130 **H** Helles	136 **Mo** Märzen/Oktoberfest	148 **Db** Doppelbock
114 **Fb** Flanders Brown	118 **Wz** Weizenbock	138 **Vl** Vienna Lager	150 **Eib** Eisbock
116 **Bs** Belgian Strong Dark Ale	120 **Bba** Belgian Black Ale	140 **Kb** Kellerbier	152 **Swb** Schwarzbier

200 **Asa** American Strong Ale		
202 **Aba** American Brown Ale	206 **Bi** Black IPA	210 **I** Imperial and Hyper Beers
204 **Ap** American Porter	208 **Bg** Barrel-aged Beers	212 **Ast** American Stout

HOW THE TABLE WORKS

Atomic number shows where to turn for more information

Atomic symbol

60 **Ss** Sweet Stout

Color indicates chapter

Beer style

HOW THE TABLE IS ORGANIZED

Each chapter runs from the lightest to the darkest beer.

KEY TO THE CHAPTERS

Ales of British or Irish Origin 1

Ales of Continental European Origin 2

Lagers of Continental European Origin 3

Beers of American Origin 4

... also indicated by colored bars on each page.

Introduction

From its illustrious history to its modern-day renaissance, beer has intrigued the masses through the ages. Craft breweries, multinational brewing companies, and novice home brewers alike use a few simple ingredients to produce pints of complexity that rival the satisfaction bestowed by any other beverage.

Beer has scope for dramatically different varieties in a rainbow of colors and a slew of heady mixtures of aromas, flavors, and textures. Yet beer remains an approachable drink—one enjoyed both a sip at a time and glass after glass. This is a drink that creates and fosters community rather than exclusivity or snobbery—a community founded on shared interests, passion for the craft of brewing, and sheer enjoyment of unique handcrafted brews. On my journey through the world of craft beer I have discovered a virtual village of people—not vying for attention or thriving on competition, but a dedicated group devoted to producing, selling, buying, sharing, and most importantly, drinking, the world's most intriguing, versatile beverage.

For centuries, beer has made the casual observer a connoisseur, the stranger a friend. This book will become your companion as you venture through the jungle of malt and hops, of stout and pilsner, of bière de garde and bock. It will give you the tools to navigate your way through the beer aisles and the confidence to build on your personal likes and dislikes to find your perfect pint.

Beer is a world to be explored at your own pace. These pages will help you wander a little less aimlessly, a little more pointedly, and will help you discover moments with beer that you never thought you would have.

I hope you enjoy this book and the beers it helps you to uncover!

MICHAEL LARSON

How to Use This Book

The **BEER SELECT-O-PEDIA** lists 90 different styles of beer (page 4). These are grouped in four chapters according to the country of origin for that style.

The periodic table makes it easy to see which types of beer you should try next: just look up a beer you know you like and find similar types nearby. At the back of the book you'll find an index of the beer styles in this book (page 216).

Each beer is graded for the same information:

- Origin
- Color of the beer (for more on the SRM, see next page).
- ABV: Alcohol By Volume—expressed as a percentage—is the world's most common way to measure the alcohol content in beer.
- IBU: International Bittering Units—the industry standard used to measure the bitterness in beer. Generally speaking, the higher the IBU the more bitter the beer will taste.

A picture of each beer will tempt your taste buds.

How to Use This Book ... continued

SRM

1	2
3	4
5	6
7-8	9-11
12-16	17-21
22-6	27-31
32-36	37+

The beers are ordered within each chapter according to where they appear in the official **STANDARD REFERENCE METHOD** (SRM) scale, which grades beer color from one (the palest yellow) to over 37 (almost black). The colors in the book are representational.

Brief descriptions of three specially **RECOMMENDED BEERS** to try in each style.

If you are cooking, it's useful to know which beers match your meal. **FOOD PAIRING SUGGESTIONS** are also indexed at the back of the book.

Each style of beer has an **ATOMIC STRUCTURE DIAGRAM** that tells you more about each beer, lists breweries to watch out for, and gives tasting notes on the style of beer.

Recommended brewers so you know who is famous for creating beers in this style.

Interesting facts about each beer that will intrigue even the most expert beer connoisseur.

The **TASTING NOTES** are divided into four groups: malt flavors, hop characteristics, fermentation, and body and mouthfeel. Sample tasting notes in each category are shown on the diagram below. For some beers, spice flavors are also notable.

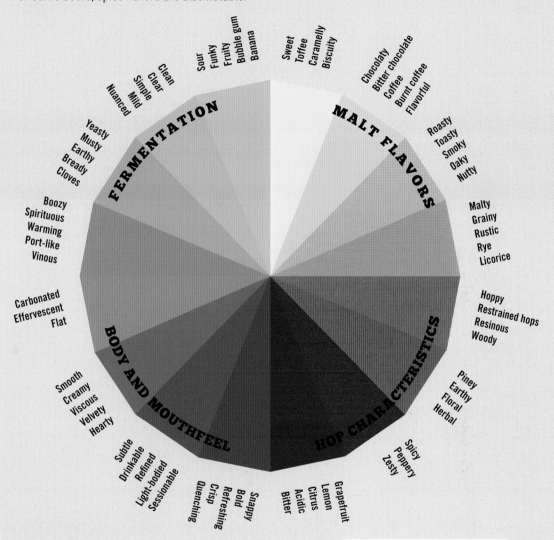

FERMENTATION

Sour
Funky
Fruity
Bubble gum
Banana

Clean
Clear
Simple
Mild
Nuanced

Yeasty
Musty
Earthy
Bready
Cloves

Boozy
Spirituous
Warming
Port-like
Vinous

Carbonated
Effervescent
Flat

MALT FLAVORS

Sweet
Toffee
Caramelly
Biscuity

Chocolaty
Bitter chocolate
Coffee
Burnt coffee
Flavorful

Roasty
Toasty
Smoky
Oaky
Nutty

Malty
Grainy
Rustic
Rye
Licorice

HOP CHARACTERISTICS

Hoppy
Restrained hops
Resinous
Woody

Piney
Earthy
Floral
Herbal

Spicy
Peppery
Zesty

Grapefruit
Lemon
Citrus
Acidic
Bitter

Snappy
Bold
Refreshing
Crisp
Quenching

BODY AND MOUTHFEEL

Smooth
Creamy
Viscous
Velvety
Hearty

Subtle
Drinkable
Refined
Light-bodied
Sessionable

Diagram to show positions of tasting notes on the **ATOMIC DIAGRAMS** in this book.

Tasting notes help you identify and enjoy the full flavor of every beer. Tasting notes appear in the same place on each page so if you know you like citrus-flavored beers you can watch out for the same symbol as you flick through the book.

Once you know what you like to taste in a beer the **TASTING NOTES** allow you to "track" that flavor through the book. This diagram shows how the icons are organized.

AN INTRODUCTION TO DRINKING BEER

Whether you are looking at it from a glass half empty or glass half full perspective, drinking beer is not a complicated process—unlike many pastimes, you don't need any expert knowledge to get started. That said, the more you know, the more you will enjoy. This section will whet your appetite before you dive into the different styles.

What is beer?

There are scores of different styles of beer, often so different from one another that it is hard to tell they are created from the same ingredients. And that is the simple beauty of this beverage. While crafted from just a few simple ingredients—water, malt, yeast, and hops—the results are hugely varied. Beers can look like sunshine or midnight. They can be clear as glass or as opaque as engine oil. They can be spritzy like champagne, viscous like maple syrup, or creamy as a milkshake.

INGREDIENTS

• **WATER** makes up the highest proportion of beer volume, generally around 90 percent. Its chemical and mineral composition has an impact on the end result, so it is crucial that the source is clean and pure. Some brewers alter the mineral content of the water to produce specific qualities in the end product.

• **MALT** begins as barley, a cereal grain grown worldwide. The origin and variety of the barley used affect the flavor profile of the beer. For use in brewing, barley must be malted, a process in which the raw grain is steeped in water until it begins to sprout and then placed into a kiln to dry. It is this process that breaks down the hard husk of the barley and changes it into a soft, usable product. Kilning occurs in a roasting drum and the temperature and length of this process governs whether the malt is light, both in color and flavor, or a dark, heavily roasted malt. A brewer chooses a particular malt in order to achieve the desired flavors and color of beer.

• **HOPS** are inextricably associated with beer—more than any other ingredient. It is surprising to some that a flower produces bitterness, and certain flavors and aromas, in beer. Hops help to preserve the beer and also provide a crucial balance to the malt, without which beer would be overly sweet and cloying. The hop plant is a vine on which small hop cones form in the late summer and early fall. There are dozens of types of hops and the brewer selects a specific variety based on the desired flavors and aromas. Hops can be spicy, citric, woody, piney, grapefruity, earthy, and/or floral. Usually hops are added during the boiling process. However, they are sometimes added later in the brewing process.

• **YEAST**, a living microorganism, is essential to brewing, as it converts the wort—the liquid produced in the early part of the brewing process—into beer. As the yeast eats the sugar in the wort, it creates a multitude of flavors—and produces alcohol. There are two commonly-used species: *Saccharomyces cerevisae*, the yeast used in ales, which ferment at warmer temperatures, and *Saccharomyces uvarum*, the yeast used in lagers, which ferment in cooler temperatures.

Ale yeast ferments more quickly than lager yeast, and upon completion of fermentation, rises to the top, hence the term "top-fermenting." By contrast, when a lager yeast has completed its task of fermentation, it settles on the bottom, and is therefore dubbed "bottom-fermenting." There are many strains within these species, each one having a different impact on the beer—some in significant and intriguing ways.

How Beer is Brewed

BREWING is where the raw ingredients are combined to form wort, to which the yeast is added, to produce beer.

The first step to making **WORT** is combining the crushed malt with hot water in the mash tun, forming the **MASH**, a porridge-like substance. During this stage, starches are broken down into sugars, and are then drawn away from the grain into the water, through what is essentially a sieve (called a lauter tun), and then into the kettle. This liquid can now officially be called wort. At this point, it is brought to a vigorous **BOIL**, which helps to sterilize the wort. Often, a beer is referred to as high or low **GRAVITY**. Gravity is a means of measuring the strength of a beer, based on the amount of malt sugars present in the wort. Generally, a high gravity beer will have a high alcohol content.

After boiling, hops are added, which help to create the bitterness, flavors, and aromas in the final product. The first additions primarily affect the bitter quality of the beer, the later additions form the aroma. Spices may be added near completion of the boil as well. Boiling continues for an hour or more, then the hops and any protein solids are removed using a strainer or a device called a whirlpool. At this point, the wort is rapidly cooled to temperatures suitable for fermentation.

FERMENTATION begins in the fermentation vessel when yeast is added to the cooled wort. Once this process is completed, the yeast is removed and the beer begins a period of rest or **MATURATION**. Most brewers use stainless steel tanks and others use oak barrels. If a beer is to be dry-hopped, hops are added directly to these vessels to sit until bottling.

Once bottled, some beers undergo a period of **CONDITIONING** or refermentation, where more yeast is added, aiding the development of carbonation in the bottle and adding further complex flavors. At the end of this process, the beer is filtered, leaving a clear brew to which carbonation is generally added immediately before bottling. However the beer has been brewed, it is now ready for packaging and shipping, to be enjoyed by beer lovers everywhere.

Current trends in brewing

The production of mass-market, light lagers is a feature of modern times. Yet creative, passionate craft brewers have continued to produce unique beers of high quality. In recent times their patience has been rewarded. The historic brews of England, Germany, and Belgium are receiving renewed and well-deserved attention, while the American styles are becoming standards in their own right. New styles are being created and established styles are being given new twists. Conservatism and caution have been thrown aside and replaced with ingenuity and brash creativity. At the same time, the classic styles of past centuries have been revived by new breweries revisiting their beer heritage.

Serving and Storing Beer

GLASSWARE

A flute for champagne and a mug for coffee. Tea in a china cup and cola in a can. Every drink seems to have its signature vessel, and beer is no exception to the rule. While Belgium takes the art of serving beer to an unprecedented level, even the most basic home-bar setup can benefit from a small makeover to the glassware department. With a few different glasses, beer can be tasted as it was intended. Some beers present best in a tall, thin cylinder, others find themselves comfortably contained in a sturdy, nonic pint glass. In almost every case, there is an ideal way for beer to be served.

• **FLUTE** Tall, slender, and stemmed, the flute typically conjures up images of wedding toasts and New Year's Eve. However, this delicate glass can be the perfect vessel for beer. The tall, thin shape is ideal for highly carbonated brews that are light in color and extremely translucent. The design tends to force the aroma upward and outward, giving the drinker a strong burst of bouquet before the first sip is taken.

• **GOBLET/CHALICE** Recommended for certain Belgian styles in particular. A glass of this type can be thin and delicate or solidly thick. It allows for splendid head retention. Many breweries produce their own customized designs.

• **IPA GLASS** This glass, marketed as recently as 2013, has yet to see wide acceptance. However, it was designed with India pale ales specifically in mind. The shape allows room for a foamy head and glass ridges aid head retention.

• **MUG/STEIN** Sturdy and with a large capacity, a mug begs for a quenching beer. The design is simple and practical, easy to use, and can hold plenty of beer.

• **PILSNER GLASS** This thin, tall, and slender glass is an ideal match for the pilsner beer for which it is named. Its height shows off the rushing stream of carbonation, while keeping

GLASSWARE

| Flute | Goblet/ chalice | Mug/ stein | IPA glass | Pilsner |

| Weizen glass | Pint/ nonic pint | Wine goblet | Tulip | Stange | Snifter |

the beer cool—a quality essential to a style best served on the cooler side. With the height to show off a bright-colored body and a brilliantly white cap, a proper pour into this glass can create a mouth-watering picture.

• **PINT/NONIC PINT** Either straight sided (pint), or with a bulge near the top (nonic pint), these glasses are the default option for many brews. The design focus is less on the drinking experience than the ease of storage. Pint glasses are cheap to make and therefore an ideal choice for many drinking establishments.

• **SNIFTER** With a slight stem and a wide bowl, this glass style is borrowed from the world of brandy. Easy to swirl, the glass gives the drinker an invitingly forward bouquet and allows the formation of "legs," which indicate the viscosity of the particular beer. Perfect for bigger, heavier, darker brews.

• **STANGE** Straight sided, this specialized glass, meaning "stick" in German, focuses the aromatics of more delicate styles of beer and helps to concentrate flavors.

• **TULIP** Its shape echoes that of the eponymous flower, the wide body narrowing near the top and then fanning out, allowing for the formation of a billowing head, harnessing and then projecting the aroma.

• **WEIZEN GLASS** With a narrow base spreading to a wider mouth, this glass is designed to enhance wheat beer. The size accommodates the desired volume of beer and the characteristic fluffy head.

• **WINE GOBLET** Another glass borrowed from beyond the world of beer, this large-bowled design can be used for a variety of beer styles. The body is wide enough to display the color and viscosity of heavier brews and, like the snifter, allows room for a fluffy head and an assertive swirl that will release the aromas easily through the wide mouth.

HOW TO STORE BEER

After you have chosen the proper glassware, there are a few easy steps to consider to maximize your tasting experience. First, ensure the beer is being stored and served at the proper temperature. Generally speaking, beer is kept best in cold, dry, dark spaces. The refrigerator is the obvious choice for many beers. Some beers should be served slightly warmer and others at cooler temperatures, but with some experimentation, these differentiations will become clear. Light, refreshing, lower alcohol beers tend to appreciate cooler temperatures, while complex, rich and dark brews may be at their best when slightly warmer. Strong, complex ales are most effectively aged in a cool, but not cold, location. A cool cellar at around 55°F (13°C) is ideal for long-term storage and can heighten and accentuate the more subtle aromas and flavors.

HOW TO POUR BEER

Pouring requires consideration, but this is another area that can be "overthought." Typically, you can achieve an adequate pour by angling the glass and pouring slowly down the side. At about two-thirds full, tilt the glass upright and finish the pour. This will help to build the head, which adds to the look, feel, and aroma of most beers.

How to Taste Beer

Tasting beer should be fun. You shouldn't be searching for proper vocabulary or awkwardly mimicking a supposed connoisseur. Your hands shouldn't sweat—your mouth should water. That said, even the most casual tasting session can be refined with a few simple steps. The brewer who crafted that lovely pint in your hand wants you to taste everything that he intended, so here are a few suggestions to help you do just that.

• **APPEARANCE** After pouring the beer into the recommended and clean glass, it is time to take it all in. When gauging its appearance take note of the color, clarity, and carbonation of the body. Also look at the head: Is it light and airy or dense and firm? Does it linger or disappear? A tall, thick head will produce more lace. Also referred to as Brussels lace, this term describes the foam left sticking to the side of the glass. Take the glass in your hand and swirl it slightly, noting the texture of the brew and its viscosity. All of this thinking time will prepare your palate for what is to come.

• **AROMA** The fragrance of a beer is a crucial element of the taste—just consider how little you can taste when your nose is blocked by a head cold. Swirl the glass to release the bouquet and, with your nose in the glass, inhale. With experience, the nuances intended by the brewer will become more apparent, but even a beginner can easily distinguish some different aromas.

• **TASTE AND MOUTHFEEL** Next, take a drink. Don't be bashful, the intention of the brewer is that you will take a mouthful, not just a nip. Wash it around on your tongue to absorb the weight and texture. Take note of the thickness, viscosity, and carbonation. All these are aspects of what is known as "mouthfeel." Finally, taste the beer and search for the initial flavors, then the center and the finish. The myriad flavors are what make beer such a consistently intriguing drink. After you swallow, you can form an overall impression. How do the pieces knit together to form the final complete tapestry of taste?

BEER TASTINGS

When tasting several beers in succession, as part of a beer dinner or a "flight" (several small servings of different beers), it is best to sample them in a particular order. Aim to try the lighter, less complex and powerful styles first, then work through your lineup toward the richer, more impactful brews. This will allow you to perceive the delicate flavors of the lighter styles before the heavier styles overshadow them. A perfect pilsner can seem watery and flavorless following a Russian imperial stout.

Pairing Food with Beer

While wine has always taken center stage at the dinner table, beer has an incredible, and generally untapped, potential. Many diners adhere to the perception that beer belongs at a bar, with a pizza, or in a plastic cup at a rowdy party. While some beers belong in these places, there have always been others with a well-earned spot at a dinner party. Fine beers, paired well, poured well, and drunk with appreciation, have the potential to pleasantly surprise and impress. The primary goal should be a marriage of beer and food resulting in a flavor experience impossible to attain with either item on its own. In essence, the sum is greater than its parts.

CHOOSING FOOD FOR BEER

Complementary pairings of beer and food aim to match similarities in both. Some obvious examples could include a light pilsner served with a summer salad or a dark Russian imperial stout served with a rich chocolate dessert. The similarities in the beer and the accompanying food create harmony and cohesion that amplify the flavors of both. A few useful tips that will help to develop complementary tasting combinations: Fatty and sweet foods do well with high alcohol beers that have hop bitterness, sweetness, or roasted malt notes. Highly carbonated beers tend to cut rich foods and cleanse the palate. At the back of the book you will find the recommended food pairings indexed by food, so you can easily find a beer to match what you are eating.

• **STYLE** In crafting a pairing, you first must know what style of beer you will be tasting.

Generally the brewer has made this an easy job, boldly emblazoning the style across the bottle. Armed with this bit of information you can look up the beer style in this book and use the atomic diagram to discover more about how it will taste (plus some recommended pairings).

• **FLAVOR FOCUS** Beer can be many things at once. It can be sweet, caramelly, malty, and heavy. It can be bitter, citric, and bright. It can be light, effervescent, and refreshingly cleansing. Attention to these individual nuances is essential when attempting to make a memorable pairing. Your taste buds have already experienced the vast array of flavors in food, it is now simply time to take note of those specifics and properly partner them with beer. A particularly effective way of doing so is to narrow down one focal point on which to build your pairing. Focus on the primary characteristic of the beer or the food with which you are attempting to pair it, and your choices become more obvious.

• **BALANCE** The backdrop to attaining a successful pairing is to consistently maintain balance. The strength and flavors in both the food and beer should create an interplay that is not dominated by either. Hearty, robust, rich foods should be matched with beers of a similar quality. Light, refreshing and delicate dishes are best suited to beers with the same characteristics. However, achieving overall balance does not mean that the pairing will necessarily involve like flavors in both beer and food. In fact, some of the most impressive beer and food pairings result from opposing flavors.

• **COMPLEMENTARY** If a beer is light, fruity and crisp, perhaps a summer salad would be a match. If it has a robust, toasty quality with a chewy malt backbone, a char-grilled steak would delight the taste buds.

- **CONTRAST** Often the best matches in food and beer are ones in which the most prominent flavor in the beer contrasts with the focal point in the food. When choosing contrasting pairings, however, you must be careful not to overdo it. A light, bright beer will be stripped of its flavors if served with a dark chocolate torte. However, a hoppy IPA will cut through the sweetness of carrot cake for a surprisingly delicious result.

THE FOOD PAIRINGS IN THIS BOOK

The recommended food pairings in this book are guided by a basic principle: Taking note of the style of beer, the focal flavor points, the beer is then paired to food with similar balance to either complement underlying flavors or contrast with them. Many pairings will have both elements and it is this interplay of flavors that creates intriguing and complex food and beer interactions.

ALES OF BRITISH OR IRISH ORIGIN

ALES OF BRITISH OR IRISH ORIGIN

Britain has had an indelible influence on modern beer styles. It is on these shoulders that so many other nations, brewers, and fantastic beers now stand. Beers with origins in Britain and Ireland that are still produced on home turf retain distinctive differences from the same historical styles that have been adapted and translated to fit a new nation's tastes. Contemporary British and Irish brewers typically still guide their brewing processes along traditional lines, making beers today that mimic styles brewed decades before.

A crucial category of British beer is bitter, considered the nation's drink of choice. After ordinary bitter comes best bitter, and then strong/extra special bitter—amped up versions with added malt and hops and increased alcohol content. For the domestic British beer drinker, the latter are the favored styles and, when in fine form, a definite English treat. While the term, "bitter," invokes images of assaulting assertive hops, bitters are well-balanced and in a camp far from the American pale ales and IPAs of such hop-based bitterness. It's not just the paler spectrum of beer on which Britain has had a notable influence. The rich English brown ale, the warming old ale and the deep, luscious porters and stouts have all been the cradles from which beers worldwide have been born.

Cask-conditioned ales remain a significant and unique ingredient of British beer culture. The United Kingdom remains one of the few nations where ale is served directly from the cask it was aged in—at cellar temperatures and with no added carbonation—and using just the natural force of gravity to conjure it from the taps. This method of serving beer is beginning to gain some momentum in other countries as well, with several official organizations championing these traditional methods worldwide. While great examples of British beers are exported to the four corners of the globe, to truly understand the greatness of these heritage-rich styles, one must experience them as they were meant to be: from the cask in a traditional pub.

North of the border, Scotland has long produced distinct ales that are as reflective of their home country as any style the world over. With a climate unsuited to growing hops, Scotland's rich, seductive ales are malt forward, complex, and warming—the perfect foil to a blustery Scottish eve. Scottish ales, sessionable and substantial, range in strength from the so-called 60-shilling to 80-shilling brews—the more expensive the better quality the beer, traditionally. Its stronger 90-shilling brother, the strong Scotch ale, or wee heavy, is a real sipper, as high in alcohol as it is in flavor, and now more commonly brewed outside the United Kingdom.

It can be argued that no country is so represented by a single brewer than Ireland. The popularization of Irish dry stout by the Guinness company has, over time, solidified into an eternal bond between a nation and a drink. It is said that no Guinness tastes so good as in Dublin at the original St. James's Gate Brewery. From that seed of brewing genius, the foreign extra stout was spawned, an export to quench the thirst of the British Empire as it explored the vast corners of the world. Ireland's other beer of note is the Irish red ale. Dubbed as such by the late beer expert and writer Michael Jackson, red ale's history and specific origin is hazy, but its fine examples are undeniably delicious.

English Golden

Origin: England
Color: 3-9 SRM
ABV: 4-5%
IBU: 40-55
Glassware: pint, nonic pint

It's often said that necessity is the mother of invention. The hot English summer of 1995 called for the popularization of this quenching brew, to rival the popularity of imported lagers.

INTENSELY QUENCHING

Also called summer ale, this refreshing beauty pours bright, light golden, and is topped with a thin layer of white. It looks perfectly refreshing—which is the intention, with a low ABV and a clean, cool hop bite. The nose is fresh and spicy. The flavor leans on the hops, but in true English fashion, still maintains a core of biscuity maltiness. After a nicely hopped, intense body, the finish is long, clean, and dry. A great summer beer served cooler than many English brews for a wonderfully thirst-quenching pint.

Three Beers to Try

SUMMER LIGHTNING   This ale from Hop Back Brewery has a nose bursting of fresh hops. It is intensely bitter but refreshing with a long, dry finish.

FULLER'S SUMMER ALE   Pale golden, crisp with a balance of biscuity malt and herby and earthy hops.

HOPHEAD   This beer from Dark Star is as it should be—clean, refreshing, and ultimately sessionable. Floral notes on both the nose and the palate keep it interesting.

Fruity

Thornbridge

Crouch Vale Brewery

John Gilbert of Hop Back Brewery invented the style in the late 1980s.

Dark Star Brewing Co.

Hop Back Brewery

Go

To compete directly with lagers, this ale was brewed to be as pale as possible.

Brooklyn Brewery

Rather than change the English breweries' focus to creating lagers, the inventors of this brew found a way to make a quenching ale, best served cold.

This style gained popularity in England during the sweltering summer of 1995.

Fuller, Smith & Turner

Refreshing

Crisp

Citric

Food Pairing

| Lightly spiced dishes | Salads | Seafood |

Ordinary Bitter

Origin: England
Color: 4-14 SRM
ABV: 3-3.9%
IBU: 20-35
Glassware: pint, nonic pint

Anything but ordinary, this English staple has a strong history and a stronger following.

SURPRISINGLY COMPLEX

A beer drinker from outside of the United Kingdom may be reluctant to order a pint of anything dubbed "ordinary," but there is very good reason to do so. The lightest in alcohol of the bitter family, this quite sessionable ale is served often—and best—from a cask in a quintessential English pub. It is slightly bitter, but with a central, often caramelly, malt character. There are surprising complexities, especially when served on cask, that come through as spicy, peppery, and even grassy hop flavors. The hops make for a quenching body and end in a dry finish, with a smooth mouthfeel throughout. There is just a thin sheath of a head, typically off-white, and an ever-so-slight level of carbonation. Color ranges from light orange to amber.

Three Beers to Try

BRAKSPEAR BITTER A soft aroma of light fruits and malts. Characteristic woody, earthy English hops carefully balance the malt, with biscuit and caramel notes.

YOUNG'S BITTER Young's number one selling beer for good reason. Very sessionable, this clean, light beer has a subtle bitter finish.

GREENE KING IPA Despite the name, the low ABV plants this brew squarely in the ordinary bitter camp. Simple, it finds a delightful balance of caramel, bready malts and floral, earthy hops

THE ATOMIC STRUCTURE OF

Ordinary Bitter

Ob

- Fruity
- Caramelly
- Greene King Brewery
- Fuller, Smith & Turner
- It was called "bitter" because of the pronounced hop bitterness compared with other ales that used to be available in England.
- Earthy
- Rogue Brewery
- In England, most ale served from a cask is a bitter.
- Wells & Young's Brewing Company
- Golding and Fuggle are the typical hop varieties used in bitter.
- Developed toward the end of the 19th century with the aim of serving beers after a shorter time in the cellar.
- Brakspear Brewing Company
- Subtle
- Some experts say the only real difference between bitter and pale ale is the way it is served: bitter on draft, pale ale in bottles.
- Adnams
- Spicy

Food Pairing

Lightly spiced Thai food	Mild English cheese	Seafood	Shepherd's pie	Bangers and mash

Best Bitter

Origin: England
Color: 5-16 SRM
ABV: 3.8-4.6%
IBU: 25-40
Glassware: pint,
nonic pint

The middle child of the bitter family, the best bitter is traditionally just that, the brewery's finest crafted brew.

A BALANCED CORE

Stuck between ordinary and extra special, this style compiles the best from both siblings, producing a remarkably drinkable, strong-but-sessionable English ale. It is generally medium gold to copper and quite clear, with a thin head that lingers just slightly above a minimally carbonated body. While maintaining an overarching theme of bitterness, it has an elevated maltiness, when compared to ordinary bitter. Best bitter can be caramelly and fruity, but is always well-balanced. At times quite filling, this beer quenches while it satisfies. A favorite in England, this delicious brew is best savored on cask at an English pub!

Three Beers to Try

ADNAMS SOUTHWOLD BITTER   With herbal hop notes throughout, this copper brew (formerly Adnams Best Bitter) has been an English classic since its birth in 1967.

YOUNG'S SPECIAL   Served almost exclusively on cask, with a loyal following, its copper body presents a bouquet of biscuit and English hops. Both aromas blend on the palate, finishing slightly bitter.

CONISTON BLUEBIRD BITTER   A great example of the style, Bluebird pours golden amber, with a thinly layered head. There are notes of caramel blended with floral hops and a dry finish.

THE ATOMIC STRUCTURE OF

Best Bitter

The greatest number of bitters produced are best bitters.

Caramelly

Greene King Brewery

Coniston Brewing Company

Also sometimes called special or premium bitter.

Earthy

Wells & Young's Brewing Company

This style is often the finest product in the brewery's overall bitter lineup.

Fresh hops

Drinkable

In England, the bitter family is most typically served on cask as a "real ale." Real ales are conditioned in the cask, imparting a light carbonation, and are served at cellar temperature—coaxing out complexities unmatched by a bottle of the same.

Brakspear Brewing Company

Rogue Brewery

Well-balanced

Adnams

Within England, specific geography plays a significant role in the prominent flavors of bitters.

Bb

Food Pairing

| Roast chicken | Curry | Bangers and mash |

Strong/Extra Special Bitter

Origin: England
Color: 6–18 SRM
ABV: 4.6-6.2%
IBU: 30–50
Glassware: pint, nonic pint

The biggest of the bitter bunch, this fine brew climbs the ABV scale, but maintains drinkability—gaining an enhanced complexity from the elevated amount of raw materials used.

CROWN JEWELS

If it were just about names, extra special bitter would get all the attention. It would be the belle of the ball and poor, old ordinary bitter would be the wallflower. But in truth, extra special stands on the shoulders of ordinary, with just enough added hops, malt, and alcohol to be fitting for the title. While the style is broad, the typical strong bitter is medium-bodied, complex, and well-balanced. They can be as light as gold or as dark as copper, and are usually capped with a layer of white foam. Despite more full hop and malt flavor than other bitters, they still come in fairly drinkable. Typically chock-full of fresh English hops, they are balanced by the rich, nutty malts so critical to a true English brew. In some, dark fruits and spice enter in both aroma and taste.

Three Beers to Try

ADNAMS BROADSIDE   Ruby red and fruity. It is bottled as "Broadside Strong Original."

YOUNG'S RAM ROD   At 5% ABV, it is categorized as an ESB and is jammed with flavor. A great blend of hops and biscuity malt, its finish is long and lingering.

FULLER'S ESB   One of the first of the style to export to America, its influence abroad is ongoing and far-reaching. A fruit-caramel blend on the nose, the body is full-flavored and bursting with

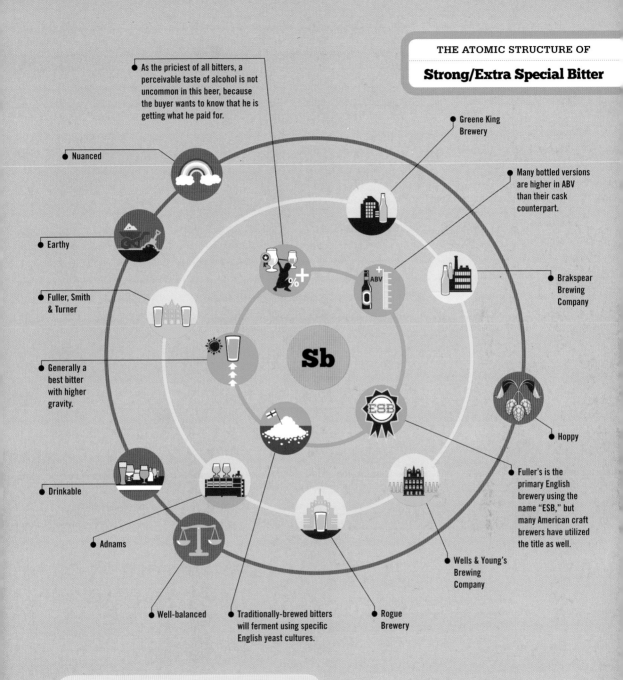

THE ATOMIC STRUCTURE OF
Strong/Extra Special Bitter

As the priciest of all bitters, a perceivable taste of alcohol is not uncommon in this beer, because the buyer wants to know that he is getting what he paid for.

Greene King Brewery

Nuanced

Many bottled versions are higher in ABV than their cask counterpart.

Earthy

Brakspear Brewing Company

Fuller, Smith & Turner

Generally a best bitter with higher gravity.

Sb

Hoppy

Fuller's is the primary English brewery using the name "ESB," but many American craft brewers have utilized the title as well.

Drinkable

Adnams

Wells & Young's Brewing Company

Well-balanced

Traditionally-brewed bitters will ferment using specific English yeast cultures.

Rogue Brewery

Food Pairing

Pork	Fried chicken	Game meats	Curry	Bangers and mash

Pale Ale

Origin: England
Color: 5–14 SRM
ABV: 3.8–6.2%
IBU: 20–50
Glassware: pint, nonic pint

Once dubbed "pale" simply because it wasn't dark, pale ale has now become a style with boundaries as wide as the world that brews it.

BITTER'S BIGGER BROTHER
English pale ale has been described as a bottled bitter. While the distinctions between these two styles can be ever so slight, there are a few. Generally, a member of the pale ale family is bigger, stronger, and more substantial than its brother in the bitter family. A glass of pale ale can be golden to deep orange to amber. The head is most consistently off-white and thin—just a fine layer remaining through the life of the pint. On the nose, sweet, caramel notes are mixed with spicy or herbal hop aromas. On first sip, there is a blend of nutty and toasted malts and a solid hop bitterness, but dark fruits, sweetness, and caramel can be present as well. Its smooth body has a lingering, clean finish. For American pale ale, see page 176.

Three Beers to Try

LONDON PRIDE   This popular Fuller's beer is a draft bitter in the United Kingdom, but a bottled pale ale elsewhere. It is earthy, full-bodied, and smooth, with nutty malts and a long, dry finish.

SAMUEL SMITH'S PALE ALE   By many standards an ESB (the lines of definition are blurred), this pale ale is brewed with water from the original well at the Old Brewery, sunk in 1758 and which is still in use.

FIRESTONE WALKER DOUBLE BARREL ALE   Firestone Walker has created a balanced beer, light on fruit

THE ATOMIC STRUCTURE OF

Pale Ale

Fruity

Clean

Earthy

Greene King Brewery

As in other English ales, Golding and Fuggle hops are typically used in pale ales.

Adnams

Pa

Fuller, Smith & Turner

The origins of the style lie in the India pale ale developed in Burton-on-Trent, England.

Some brewers "Burtonize" the water by adding gypsum to make the ale more like those brewed in Burton-on-Trent.

Firestone Walker Brewing Company

Not truly "pale" in color, it was so named when compared to the other popular styles of the age: porter and stout.

Herbal

Spicy

The differences between bitter and pale ale are slight, but typically pale ales will be slightly more heavily hopped.

Samuel Smith Old Brewery

Food Pairing

| English cheese | Grilled meats | Cream-based pasta dishes | Fish and chips |

India Pale Ale

Origin: England
Color: 6-14 SRM
ABV: 4.5-7.5%
IBU: 40-60
Glassware: pint, nonic pint

IPAs have become a significant feature of the craft beer world. English IPAs, however, differ greatly from their American cousins.

HOPS AND MORE HOPS

With a past littered with myth and legend, the truth about India pale ale's history is hazy. As a thirsty beer drinker, however, you only need to know a few simple things. It is hoppy—generously, bitterly, and sometimes assaultingly so. The English style of IPA is earthy, spicy, and herbal, with a solid malt backbone that, while obviously present, takes a backseat to the hops. In fine examples, the hops aren't simple, but layered with distinct spice—separate, but working in perfect orchestration and harmony. It is scented with spice and herbal hops, yet also has an undercurrent of malt. English IPAs can be intensely bitter with a long, lingering finish.

Three Beers to Try

SAMUEL SMITH'S INDIA ALE   Primarily focused on balance, it is not overly hopped, but is malty and earthy with notes of tart fruit. It is light bodied and dry, with a bitter lingering finish.

FULLER'S INDIA PALE ALE   Deep golden with a sticky, lacing head. Caramel and earthy hops on the nose transition through the palate, adding a balanced backdrop of sweet malts.

GOOSE ISLAND INDIA PALE ALE   Made with half American hops and half English, this American IPA still fits the British style. Herbal and spicy up front it leads to a malty center and a

THE ATOMIC STRUCTURE OF
India Pale Ale

Ipa

Meantime Brewing Company

Brooklyn Brewery

Some believe the precursor to IPA was October beer, a brew made to be aged up to 18 months— perfect for drinking after the 6-month voyage to India.

Earthy

Burton ale was one of England's most popular styles until the late 1940s.

Harviestoun Brewery

Sweeter and darker than its cousin, IPA, Burton ale gradually disappeared from sale.

Goose Island Beer Co.

George Hodgson of Bow Brewery, London, was one of the biggest suppliers of IPA until he fell out of favor with the East India Trading Company.

Samuel Smith Old Brewery

Herbal

It is called India pale ale due to its popularity in the British colonies in India.

Spicy

Bitter

Fuller, Smith & Turner

Food Pairing

| Spicy food | Carrot cake | Thai food | Curry | Aged cheddar |

Light/Pale Mild

**Origin: England
Color: 8-17 SRM
ABV: 2.8-5%
IBU: 10-20
Glassware: pint,
nonic pint**

The characteristic thread of English maltiness weaves its way through this style, but the tell-tale hops of the bitter family manifest here slightly softer and more restrained.

ENGLAND'S OLD FAVORITE

What used to be a house favorite, on tap at every pub across the English countryside in the 1960s, has seen drastic decline in the last several decades. This softer, less hoppy brew has relinquished much of its former following to bitters. However, these low-alcohol, light-colored ales are perfect session brews and still have a place in the English beer family. They have experienced a recent resurgence and are quite fittingly served on cask. Without a great variety of specific distinctions, this style is pleasant, often with lightly fruity notes mixing harmoniously with the soft, English-style hops. The malt backbone is consistent and sturdy, without being overpowering.

Three Beers to Try

TIMOTHY TAYLOR'S GOLDEN BEST Light amber and clear, a slight aroma of bready malts mix with fruit. Light in body, it is refreshing and quaffable.

BRAKSPEAR OXFORD GOLD The golden body opens with a fresh bouquet of citrus and the soft texture eases to a fruity finish.

O'HANLON'S YELLOWHAMMER A blend of floral and citrus hops, this simple straightforward golden-colored beer

THE ATOMIC STRUCTURE OF

Light/Pale Mild

Lm

Simple

Milds were often associated with the working class.

O'Hanlon's Brewing Company

Milds are also sometimes referred to as "running beers." This stems from the fact that they are young beers, which are not aged for long periods.

Brakspear Brewing Company

Sessionable

At their advent, milds were typically stronger than the brewery's bitter. They have since become known as the lowest-strength in the lineup.

Greene King Brewery

This type of mild is more often found in the northern parts of England.

Coopers Brewery

Timothy Taylor & Co.

Lightly hoppy

Restrained hops

Before specific separation of "mild" as a style, the term was applied to many beers that were not aged or stored.

The Inveralmond Brewery

Food Pairing

| Shellfish | Salad | Light chicken dishes | Curry |

Irish Red Ale

Origin: Ireland
Color: 9-18 SRM
ABV: 4-6%
IBU: 17-28
Glassware: pint, nonic pint

This brew has mostly been overshadowed by stout, Ireland's signature style. But the lesser-known Irish red ale deserves a place on any beer lover's list.

WARM COLOR, RICH FLAVOR

With its rich red pour, one can immediately see this beer's potential. The color is a hearty blend of bronze, amber, and even edges of blood orange. The head is an advertisement for the malt, looking rich, frothy, and tan. And yet, an undercurrent of light, earthy hops comes off on the nose as well. From the scent to the body and taste, this brew is a well-rounded, balanced treat. It has decent body and a moderate level of carbonation followed by a typically roasted, dry finish. On the palate, there are light hops and toasted or caramel notes in many examples of the style. It's an easy-drinking pint, one that can be enjoyed with a warm, hearty meal, or as a meal itself.

Three Beers to Try

BRIAN BORU OLD IRISH RED   Named after an Irish king, this ale from the Three Floyds Brewing Company is indeed a royal brew. A blended balance of caramel notes and citrus.

GREAT LAKES CONWAY'S IRISH ALE
Bright amber in color, toasty, caramelly, and bready. Named after the brewery owner's grandfather.

SMITHWICK'S IMPORTED PREMIUM IRISH ALE   Pours light mahogany and drinks smooth, it was originally brewed in St. Francis Abbey Brewery in Kilkenny, Ireland.

Caramelly

Carlow Brewing company

Murphy Brewery Ireland

While it is still brewed in Ireland, American brewers have also latched on to this style.

Some beers classified as Irish red ales are actually brewed like a lager.

Toasty

Evolved from the bitter/pale ale family.

Ir

Smithwick's (Guinness & Co.)

Hearty

Beer writer Michael Jackson was the first to define this brew as a distinct style.

Rich

Great Lakes Brewing Company

Sessionable

First brewed in the Irish town of Kilkenny in 1710 by what is now known as Smithwick's Brewery.

Three Floyds Brewing Company

Food Pairing

Pork	Shepherd's pie	Beef stew

Scottish Ales

Origin: Scotland
Color: 9–17 SRM
ABV: 2.5–5%
IBU: 10–30
Glassware: pint, nonic pint, thistle

Sociable beers with subtle nuances, Scottish ales are founded on smooth, rich maltiness.

MAKING THE MOST OF THE CLIMATE

Typically pouring amber to dark ruby, a pint of Scottish ale screams malt. And for good reason: Scotland's climate precludes the growth of hops, naturally encouraging brewers to accentuate what is more easily available. A solid crown of off-white to tan laces down the glass. The base is solidly set on the malts, with some examples displaying notes of caramel, light chocolate, vanilla, dark fruits, sweetness, and sometimes even slight smokiness. A medium body makes for a sessionable yet substantial brew, perfectly matched for cool weather. A finish of light hops bitterness is not uncommon— enough for balance, but generally understated. The ales are traditionally classified "60/-" or "light;" "70/-" or "heavy;" "80/-" or "export." The number refers to the price (see opposite). For "90/-" ales also called "wee heavy," turn to strong Scotch ale on page 42.

Three Beers to Try

80 SHILLING   Belhaven Brewery's bright bronze-amber ale has a nice off-white head. This is an easy drinker with a blend of sweet malt and a light background of hops.

DARK ISLAND   Dark red-brown with a well-layered nose of roast malt, chocolate, earth, and slight peat, this lightly hopped Orkney Brewery beer has a dry finish.

ROBERT THE BRUCE   This Three Floyds brew pours ruby, with a sticky beige head. It is well-balanced and smooth, but caramel and a significant roastiness add to a complex experience

Caramelly

Traquair House Brewery

Wells & Young's Brewing Company

Originally, Scottish ales were distinguished by price—for example, an ale called "80/-," cost 80 shillings per barrel.

Longer, cooler fermentations are common in this style.

Malty

Mac

With the absence of native hops, early brewers used various spices to balance the malt.

Belhaven Brewery

Substantial

Due to the cool climate, hops cannot easily grow in Scotland. As a result, most Scottish beers emphasize malt.

The Orkney Brewery

Rich

Another ale of Scottish descent, the rare heather ale, is one of the world's oldest styles.

Three Floyds Brewing Company

Food Pairing

| Lamb chops | Mild cheeses | Roast beef | Game birds |

English Barley Wine

Origin: England
Color: 8–22 SRM
ABV: 8–12%
IBU: 35–70
Glassware: snifter

Big and bold, yet also subtle and soft, barley wines are the perfect contradiction and make a beautiful evening sipper.

MOUTH-FILLING AND MALTY

Prepare yourself. With ABV of up to 12 percent and complexities in every category, barley wines can be unexpected and delicious. The colors vary, but typically it is medium-dark, with some examples starting on the orange side of amber and others creeping toward mahogany. It has a bit of a head, but not one to linger, and veils, just for a moment, the blend of incredible aromas below—from caramel to dark fruits, spices, apples, toffee, and oak. The palate can show just as vast an array, with a mouthfeel that is smooth, coating, and chewy. There is a balance, but typically the malt nuances shine.

Three Beers to Try

O'HANLON'S THOMAS HARDY'S ALE
Brewed just once a year, and said to withstand aging of up to 25 years, this brew, which has gone in and out of production, is much sought-after by beer lovers. It has notes of dark fruit and a port-like viscosity.

HARVEST ALE   Brewed just once a year, by J.W. Lees to commemorate the Maris Otter barley harvest, this vintage ale has maple syrup sweetness with a malty backbone and fruit notes.

OLD FOGHORN ALE   The forerunner for the style in America, this brew is crafted in the English style and dry-hopped with Cascade hops by the Anchor Brewing Company.

Fruity

Sweet

Firestone Walker Brewing Company

Anchor Brewing Company

The term barley wine was probably first used by brewers due to their high regard for wine.

This beer has many similarities to the English old ale (page 44).

Traquair House Brewery

Warming

Bar

This beer ages well.

Weyerbacher Brewing Company

Creamy

The brewer Bass was probably the first to officially describe a beer as barley wine. Its No.1 strong ale was given this tag in 1903.

J.W. Lees & Co.

Complex

A great after-dinner beverage choice.

O'Hanlon's Brewing Company

Food Pairing

Stilton cheese	Bread pudding	Hearty foods	Goat cheese	Crème brûlée

Strong Scotch Ale

Origin: Scotland
Color: 14–25 SRM
ABV: 6.5–10%
IBU: 17–35
Glassware: thistle, tulip, snifter

Also known as "wee heavy," this ale has a thick, creamy mouthfeel and layer upon layer of rich malts. It is a beer that stands alone and makes a perfect after-dinner sipper.

SWEET WITHOUT BEING CLOYING

As the glass fills up you can tell it is a rich, sweet, undeniably intriguing brew. Aromas of toffee, malt, fruits, and caramel are common and mouth-watering. The head is dense and tan and sits on a body of copper to deep brown, with edges and accents of amber. The mouthfeel is full-bodied, juicy, and often viscous, but with just a slight bite of hops to avoid an unpleasant cloying feel. The relatively high alcohol content is warming and appropriately gauged to keep the drinker to a pace that ensures pure enjoyment without excess.

Three Beers to Try

BELHAVEN WEE HEAVY This ale has an aroma laden with layers, from vanilla to rich malts and earth. Dry on the palate, it is on the lighter side for the style.

DIRTY BASTARD On the hoppier side for the style, but this brew from the Founders Brewing Company is still richly full of malt character and an intriguing finish.

SKULL SPLITTER Produced by the Orkney Brewery, this ale is well-balanced, smooth, creamy, and dry. It is named for the 7th Viking Earl of Orkney—and maybe for its 8.5% ABV.

THE ATOMIC STRUCTURE OF
Strong Scotch Ale

Caramelly

Broughton Ales

Toffee

The soft water of Scotland is well-suited to the malt-forward, strong Scotch ale.

A perfect after-dinner drink.

Traquair House Brewery

The Orkney Brewery

We

Also called 90/- (90 shilling) or "wee heavy."

Founders Brewing Company

Rich

Scotch ale yeast works at around 55°F (13°C), rather than the traditional ale yeast which works at around 65°F (18°C).

55°F

The Caledonian Brewery Company

Viscous

Belhaven Brewery

Food Pairing

Heavy desserts	Crème brûlée	Mild cheese	Game	Short ribs

English Old Ale

Origin: England
Color: 10–30 SRM
ABV: 4.5–6%
IBU: 30–60
Glassware: snifter, pint

Old ale has become a catch-all category for many sweet and complex beers, but was historically a beer of higher than normal alcohol content, aged to achieve a myriad of complexities.

A RICH AND INTRIGUING BREW

Likely a descendent of the historic Burton ale, old ales tend to be sweeter and darker than barley wines, with less hopping. In color, they vary widely, from pale amber to dark ruby. They have layers of flavor that span the palate: treacle, raisins, dark fruits, nuts, chocolate and molasses in the darker versions, and tart fruit and spicy hops in the lighter. Often sherry and port-like notes appear in both flavor and feel and hints of leather and tobacco further intensify the experience. The texture is critical and often intriguing. Chewy, vinous and intense, old ales can make for great, sipping brews, that finish with an alcoholic warmth.

Three Beers to Try

OLD PECULIER   The yardstick of the style, this beer by Theakston is a mix of sweet caramel, dark fruits, and chocolate. Earthy hops balance the malts and it finishes dry.

FULLER'S 1845   On the heavier side of the alcohol spectrum for the style, this one is still quite drinkable. Dark fruits and caramel suspend over a body of sweet, bready malt and light hops.

GREENE KING OLDE SUFFOLK ALE
Medium brown with ruby edges, the malty core has hints of dark fruits and toffee. A slight, but present layer of earthy hops throughout.

THE ATOMIC STRUCTURE OF

English Old Ale

Dark fruity esters

Sweet

Greene King Brewery

Marston's Beer Company

This style typically ages wonderfully and makes for interesting comparisons after periods of cellaring.

Vinous

A close kin to barley wine.

Harviestoun Brewery

Eo

Also known as stock, strong, or stale ale.

Samuel Smith Old Brewery

Originally, much of the character of old ales came from the *Brettanomyces* yeast present in the barrels.

Chewy

Fuller, Smith & Turner

T&R Theakston

Traditionally used as stock ale to blend with a younger beer before serving.

Food Pairing

| Roast beef | Roast game | Stilton cheese | Serve as a digestif |

English Strong Old Ale

Origin: England
Color: 8-22 SRM
ABV: 6.5-12%
IBU: 20-75
Glassware: snifter

In many ways similar to English barley wine, English strong old ale takes on a darker hue and a rich, malty character.

BIG, BOLD, AND SATISFYING

While distinct differences separate English barley wine and English old ale, this style toes the line, borrowing characteristics from both of its sister styles. Dark like old ale, but strong like barley wine, the end result is a palpable depth and complexity. Hops are typically slight, but perhaps present as an earthy bitterness. There can be a fruitiness that lends to the mix of flavors as well as a big malty sweetness. Varied notes of caramel, vanilla, raisins, plums, wood, earth, and spices are just a few of the many potential nuances found in this style. Overall, rich and viscous, these deliciously big brews are practically a meal in themselves!

Three Beers to Try

GALE'S PRIZE OLD ALE Sherry-like notes on the palate, along with dark fruits and earthy tones. A perfect beer with which to compare different vintages in a vertical tasting.

SAMUEL SMITH'S YORKSHIRE STINGO
Aging over a year in oak barrels, Stingo develops flavors of raisins, caramel, dark fruits and light oak. Complex and sophisticated.

FULLER'S VINTAGE ALE Individually boxed and numbered, it feels more like a gift than a beer. And yet, it's both. Balanced beautifully with toasted malts, light caramel, citrus, and a

Originally, higher amounts of alcohol were mainly used for the preservative effects on the beer.

Dark fruits

Boozy

Samuel Smith Old Brewery

Many versions of this style are bottle-conditioned.

George Gale & Co.

Malty

Also known around the world as English strong ale.

Ridgeway Brewing

Strong old ales went through a dip in popularity in the late 1800s, when the English tax system imposed increased levies on beers with higher alcohol content.

Thornbridge Brewery

Complex

Old ales may have their roots in Burton ale.

Wychwood Brewery Company

Fuller, Smith & Turner

Es

Food Pairing

| Heavy stews | Grilled game meats | Stilton cheese | Rich desserts |

Winter Warmer

Origin: England
Color: 18–22 SRM
ABV: 5–7.5%
IBU: 30–50
Glassware: pint

The aroma of gingerbread, mulling spices, and freshly baked treats evoke images of warm fires and holiday tidings. A winter warmer is a beer fitting for just such a time.

COOKIES AND SPICE

Nutmeg, cinnamon, cloves, and allspice. While it may sound like a recipe for Christmas cookies or festive bread, it is actually the list of spices you may encounter on the bouquet and palate of a winter warmer. The style is most often dark in color, ranging from deep amber to dark brown and topped with a well-suited beige head. The inviting nose is a well-crafted blend of spices, mixed with malts and typically lacking any hoppiness. Winter warmers are rich in mouthfeel and flavor, a chewy maltiness and scattered dark fruits are not uncommon.

Three Beers to Try

JUBELALE   A surprisingly hoppy version by Deschutes, the malty core has blends of dark fruits, earthy chocolate, and spice.

WINTER SOLSTICE SEASONAL ALE   The aroma tells of a sweet, caramel, spicy palate. This brew by Anderson Valley is smooth and well-balanced.

BRRR SEASONAL ALE   A bitter introduction comes through as pine, grass, and citrus. The maltiness stands strong, but this one is hop forward in true all-American style. Produced by Widmer

THE ATOMIC STRUCTURE OF

Winter Warmer

The yeast used in this style can vary dramatically, from Belgian strains to clean lager ones.

Deschutes Brewery

Widmer Brothers Brewing

Some versions of winter warmers more akin to the English style, may fall into the old ale category.

Anchor Brewing Company

Odell Brewing Co.

Cloves

Is sometimes placed as a sub-style under English old ale.

Malty

Anderson Valley Brewing Company

Ww

Cinnamon

Rich

Anchor Brewing Company has released a different version of their Christmas ale every year since 1975.

Great Lakes Brewing Company

Nutmeg

Winter warmers are not to be confused with holiday ales—a category indicating a time period of release, not a specific style.

Spiced

Food Pairing

| Roast meats | Robust cheeses | Spiced desserts | Apple pie |

Dark Mild

Origin: England
Color: 15-34 SRM
ABV: 2.8-5%
IBU: 10-25
Glassware: pint, nonic pint

As a low-gravity beer, sessionable but well-built, dark milds are the perfect accompaniment to a hearty lunch.

PLEASINGLY MELLOW

In true English beer-naming fashion, mild is an understated style. With a low ABV, but still flavorful and solid, this beer becomes the perfect choice for many occasions. This mellow, almost flat, porter-colored brew is a chameleon of style. It is said that "if the brewer calls it a mild—then, by Jove, it is." Generally speaking, hops are on the light side and malts are prevalent, bringing roasty, chocolaty notes. The best of the dark mild family are low in alcohol, but still flavorful, rich, and interesting beers.

Three Beers to Try

GALE'S FESTIVAL ALE A well-awarded beer, Gale's is a complex blend of raisins and citrus in a full-bodied mild of 4.8% ABV.

SARAH HUGHES DARK RUBY MILD
Pouring a deep brown with ruby edges, it is fruity and strong for the style. Complex and, when well-paired, a perfect food companion.

GOOSE ISLAND MILD WINTER   Light brown and capped with a nice creamy off-white head, the aroma is bready with dark fruits and a rich caramel malt palate.

THE ATOMIC STRUCTURE OF

Dark Mild

Caramelly

The Orkney Brewery

Wychwood Brewery

Dark milds were considered low-strength versions of porters when the porter/stout style was differentiating.

Roasty

Moorhouse's Brewery

Flavorful

Were preferred by the working class due to their satisfying, yet sessionable quality

Mi

Goose Island Beer Co.

A staple in northern English pubs, milds made up 61% of the ale sold in England in the 1960s, but have since dwindled.

Mild was named as such because it was lighter-bodied and less aged than those beers with which it was mixed.

Sarah Hughes Brewery

Light bodied

Refreshing

George Gale & Co.

Food Pairing

| Barbecue | Cured meats | Meat sandwiches | Mushroom dishes | Cassoulet |

English Brown Ale

Origin: England
Color: 12–35 SRM
ABV: 3–5.5%
IBU: 12–30
Glassware: pint, nonic pint

Originally a working man's brew, brown ale has now found favor with beer lovers from all walks of life.

LIGHT AND DARK

A brown ale is for those on the fence. Less weighty than a porter, but more toasty and malty than a pale ale, brown ales have settled comfortably into a between-ales niche in beerland. The range in color within this style is significant, from a translucent light brown, almost amber, to a rich, hearty brown, almost black. These differences stem from geography: the darker brews come from the south of England and the lighter come from the north. In both styles, however, the malts steal the show, with just a hint of hops in most examples. With this comes toasty flavors and nuttiness, caramel, and even fruit.

Three Beers to Try

SAMUEL SMITH'S NUT BROWN ALE Rich amber with mahogany edges, this ale has a nutty character and deep maltiness. It is dry throughout and has a slightly fruity finish.

NEWCASTLE BROWN ALE Produced by Heineken and nicknamed "Newkie," it has become the most popular bottled English beer. Crafted in the traditional style, blending an amber and a darker brown to achieve the classic style of the final product.

TURBODOG Dark brown, malty, and rich, this brew produced by Abita has notes of sweet chocolate and toffee interspersed through a medium body.

THE ATOMIC STRUCTURE OF

English Brown Ale

Bn

Caramelly

Nutty

After a period of dormancy of about 100 years, London brewer Manns revived the name "brown ale" in the early 1900s.

Toasty

Malty

Lost Coast Brewery

Newcastle Brown Ale was created in 1928, after three years of development.

Northern England's browns are higher in alcohol and lighter in color.

Heineken

Samuel Smith Old Brewery

Abita Brewing Company

The color comes primarily from two malts used in the brewing process: caramel and chocolate malts.

The Caledonian Brewery Company

Southern England's browns are lower in alcohol and darker in color.

Brooklyn Brewery

Food Pairing

| Roasted meats | Hearty dishes | Beef stew | Pork loin |

English Porter

Origin: England
Color: 20-30 SRM
ABV: 4-5.5%
IBU: 18-40
Glassware: pint,
nonic pint

The original choice of London's transport workers was a blend of three beers. The style has changed constantly since its advent and remains ambiguous even today.

A VARIED STYLE

From a light chestnut to a black-edged deep brown, English porters have a vast and varied style guideline. Generally less full-bodied than a stout, some push even this boundary. Typically an off-white head may approach tan, and generally has decent weight and retention. The texture is soft and smooth, with just enough carbonation to leave a dry, malty, bready finish. In many examples there are caramel, toffee, chocolate, and light coffee notes—all blended eloquently with the malt core. With its reasonably light alcohol content, this is a perfect partner for hearty dinners of grilled and roasted meat.

Three Beers to Try

TADDY PORTER This Samuel Smith beer pours almost black, the bouquet is a mosaic of caramel, chocolate, and dark fruits. The fruity nose becomes a tang on the tongue and finishes dry.

MEANTIME LONDON PORTER The tan head settles to a one-finger puff atop a ruby and chestnut body. Light fruits and a well-balanced sweetness end in a fairly dry finish.

FULLER'S LONDON PORTER Dark brown with amber edges and an intense balance of hops and malt. Bitterness rounds out the complex and varied malt. Smooth.

THE ATOMIC STRUCTURE OF

English Porter

- Caramelly
- Toffee
- Chocolaty
- Darwin Brewery
- Porter's popularity has gone through ebbs and flows, becoming almost extinct around the time of World War I.
- Nutty
- Considered the first industrialized beer.
- Harviestoun Brewery
- Roasty
- Guinness, now most famous for its stouts, at one time brewed only porter.

Ep

1700?

- Meantime Brewing Company
- The original English porter was a blend of three beers: an old, aged ale, a new ale, and a mild ale.
- Samuel Smith Old Brewery
- Fuller, Smith & Turner
- While probably created around 1700, porter didn't gain that name until almost 50 years later.
- St. Peter's Brewery

Food Pairing

Roasted foods	Light chocolate desserts	Burgers	Steak	Sausages

Baltic Porter

**Origin: England
Color: 17–30 SRM
ABV: 5.5–9.5%
IBU: 20–40
Glassware: pint,
nonic pint, mug**

Originally brewed in England, this beer was exported to countries in the Baltic and Scandinavia, and then adopted by its recipients and crafted into what it is today.

A HARDY TRAVELER

This dark, smooth beauty was brewed bigger and bolder in order to survive the journey from England to the Baltic countries. Since the original journey, however, it has become a distinct, stand-alone style. Dark mahogany to black, it is smooth, full-bodied, and almost coating—nearing stout in character. Typically brewed as a lager, the malt-forward introduction can be a bevy of flavors: caramel, chocolate, roasty notes, licorice, raisins, prunes, and molasses. There is no flavor from the hops, but a balance and a bitterness is attained in their presence. It is sweet on the finish and overall a velvety treat. Unknown to many, Baltic porters are worth discovering.

Three Beers to Try

SINEBRYCHOFF PORTER   Brewed by Scandinavia's oldest operating brewery. It is silky smooth and intense. Dark fruits, brown sugar, and warming alcohol end in a roasty finish.

OKOCIM PORTER   From Poland, an opaque black with a light brown, solid head. Smooth, slightly boozy with a semisweet, fruity finish.

BALTIKA #6 PORTER   Highly praised, it is brewed according to traditional English recipes. Sweet malts, chocolate, and slightly burnt roastiness throughout.

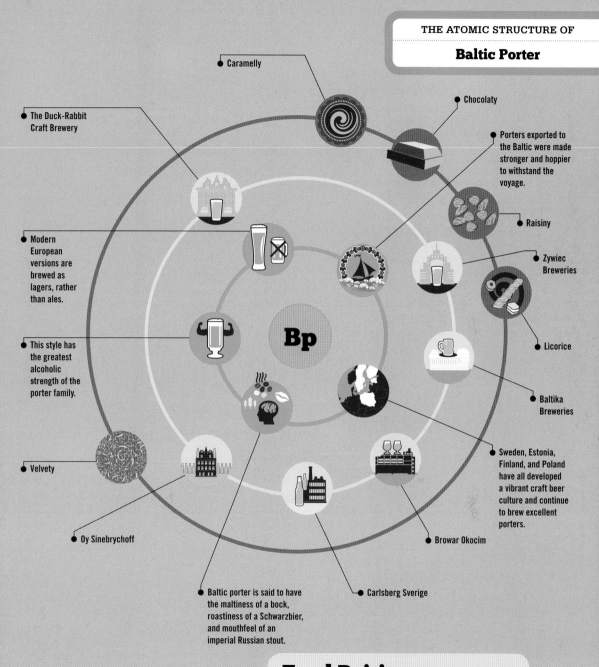

Caramelly

Chocolaty

The Duck-Rabbit Craft Brewery

Porters exported to the Baltic were made stronger and hoppier to withstand the voyage.

Modern European versions are brewed as lagers, rather than ales.

Raisiny

Zywiec Breweries

This style has the greatest alcoholic strength of the porter family.

Licorice

Bp

Baltika Breweries

Velvety

Sweden, Estonia, Finland, and Poland have all developed a vibrant craft beer culture and continue to brew excellent porters.

Oy Sinebrychoff

Browar Okocim

Baltic porter is said to have the maltiness of a bock, roastiness of a Schwarzbier, and mouthfeel of an imperial Russian stout.

Carlsberg Sverige

Food Pairing

| Barbecue | Chocolate cake | Roasted meats |

Irish Dry Stout

Origin: Ireland
Color: 25-40+ SRM
ABV: 4-5%
IBU: 30-45
Glassware: pint,
nonic pint, mug

This style was refined and typified in Ireland, and today few beers are so closely tied to a single nation.

ROASTED BARLEY

Simply the mention of dry stout conjures images of Irish pubs and Arthur Guinness. Evolving from the porters brewed in London, stouts were stronger and more full-bodied. Dry stout is typified by the use of roasted barley instead of black roasted malt. This gives the characteristic core of sharp, espresso-like roastiness. It is an opaque deep brown to pure motor-oil black with a thick, creamy head. There can be a hint of hop bitterness, but this is usually overcome by the bitterness of dark chocolate, cocoa, or coffee. From a cask or a can with a nitrogen widget, the creaminess makes this brew smooth and chewy. Deceivingly refreshing and highly sessionable, Irish dry stout is known to be the perfect choice for a long evening in the pub.

Three Beers to Try

GUINNESS DRAUGHT STOUT   The world's most famous dry stout. The fluffy brownish head is the focal point. On first sip, there is an almost burnt bitter espresso flavor.

BEAMISH IRISH STOUT   Beamish makes a dry stout that is creamy, toasty, and light. With a bitter, coffee and dark chocolate center, the finish is dry and refreshing.

MURPHY'S IRISH STOUT   Deep brown with mahogany edges, this stout has a stiff, tan cap. It is mildly dry, mellow, and much less aggressive than other famous examples of this style.

THE ATOMIC STRUCTURE OF

Irish Dry Stout

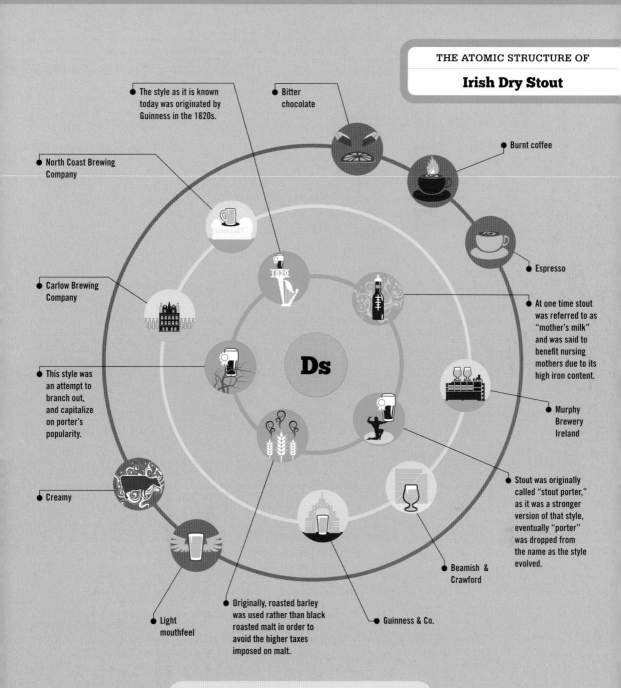

The style as it is known today was originated by Guinness in the 1820s.

Bitter chocolate

Burnt coffee

North Coast Brewing Company

Espresso

Carlow Brewing Company

At one time stout was referred to as "mother's milk" and was said to benefit nursing mothers due to its high iron content.

This style was an attempt to branch out, and capitalize on porter's popularity.

Ds

Murphy Brewery Ireland

Creamy

Stout was originally called "stout porter," as it was a stronger version of that style, eventually "porter" was dropped from the name as the style evolved.

Beamish & Crawford

Light mouthfeel

Originally, roasted barley was used rather than black roasted malt in order to avoid the higher taxes imposed on malt.

Guinness & Co.

Food Pairing

| Oysters | Seared scallops | Beef stew | Chocolate soufflé |

Sweet Stout

Origin: England
Color: 30-40+ SRM
ABV: 3-6%
IBU: 15-40
Glassware: pint, nonic pint, mug, snifter

While the health effects of beer are rarely touted today, not long ago sweet stout was marketed as just that—a nutritious choice for the masses.

SWEET AND COMFORTING

This one pours deep, oily, and opaque. Its intimidating black color seems to bid the drinker beware. In contrast, the aroma is inviting, with sweet maltiness and creamy, burnt sugar notes rising from the glass and light layers of vanilla, chocolate, dark fruit, and coffee are not uncommon. After a sip, inhibitions are gone—it is a comforting brew with a viscous mouthfeel meant for sipping, but an ABV that allows for a few pints at a time. The addition of milk sugar, or lactose, counters the dry mouthfeel of other stouts. Initially an alternative to bitter dry stouts or boozy Russian imperials, sweet stout still finds its niche drinker today.

Three Beers to Try

ST. PETER'S CREAM STOUT Bitter and burnt, with notes of espresso and dark chocolate, its mouthfeel is soft and creamy, finishing in a full circle at bittersweet.

LEFT HAND MILK STOUT Pours ultra-black with a nice ecru head. Velvety aromas of vanilla and chocolate lead you to believe dessert has arrived. And it has.

YOUNG'S DOUBLE CHOCOLATE STOUT While the category of this beer is debatable, the verdict is not. A big beer with complexities in flavor and mouthfeel. Blends of cream, bittersweet chocolate, and a light coffee finish.

THE ATOMIC STRUCTURE OF

Sweet Stout

The perceived health benefits of milk stout led some doctors to prescribe it as a cure for illness in the 1900s.

The Duck-Rabbit Craft Brewery

Sweet

Bittersweet chocolate

The inability of yeast to ferment lactose creates a smooth and creamy sweetness.

Roasty

Three Floyds Brewing Company

The Boston Beer Company

Sweet stout was born in 1875, when John Henry Johnson received a patent for a beer consisting of barley, hops, whey, and lactose.

St. Peter's Brewery

In the 1940s, the term "milk" used to advertise stout was prohibited in the United Kingdom as misleading.

Creamy

Viscous

Also called milk stout and cream stout.

Left Hand Brewing Company

Wells & Young's Brewing Company

Ss

1875

Food Pairing

| Short ribs | Mexican mole-based dishes | Ice cream | Chocolate |

Oatmeal Stout

Origin: England
Color: 22–40+ SRM
ABV: 3.8–6%
IBU: 20–40
Glassware: pint, nonic pint, mug

A bowl of piping-hot oatmeal can be a comforting morning ritual. The addition of oats to stout has the same effect, creating a soft, creamy, and delicious beer.

ADDED CREAMINESS

In brewing, it's the simplest, sometimes seemingly insignificant, changes that can entirely shift the final product. The addition of oats to stout is just such an example. Adding a rich creaminess, the mouthfeel is soft and the flavors complex. The roastiness becomes rounded around the edges, and the dryness of other beers within this style becomes slightly sweeter. There can be notes of dark chocolate, roastiness, dark fruits, and even nuttiness, but the mouthfeel steals the show. Creamy, smooth, and soft, this brew seems made to accompany dessert.

Three Beers to Try

SAMUEL SMITH'S OATMEAL STOUT
This brew revitalized the style in 1980. Pours black with deep reddish edges. Silky smooth, hints of bittersweet chocolate, and a dry finish.

YOUNG'S OATMEAL STOUT Pouring a deep brown, the soft nose is an intriguing blend of light, earthy hops and dark chocolate. Creamy smooth mouthfeel and dryish finish.

ROGUE SHAKESPEARE OATMEAL STOUT A creamy head crowns a deep brown body. The sip is smooth, chocolaty, and roasty with a tinge of citrus on the finish.

THE ATOMIC STRUCTURE OF
Oatmeal Stout

Pairs nicely with chocolate chip cookies.

McAuslan Brewing

Chocolaty

Elysian Brewing Company

An overuse of oats in the brewing process can lead to poor head retention.

Anderson Valley Brewing Company

In the late 1800s, oats were perceived as a healthy addition to beer.

Os

Creamy

Rogue Brewery

Smooth

Brewing with oats can be difficult, as the consistency in the mash can become sticky.

Rich

Wells & Young's Brewing Company

Oats are a staple crop in Britain, and this adjunct found its initial place in brewing there during the Middle Ages.

Soft

Samuel Smith Old Brewery

Food Pairing

| Chocolate desserts | Ice cream | Rich fruit desserts | Cheesecake |

Foreign/Extra Stout

Origin: Ireland
Color: 30–40+ SRM
ABV: 5.5–8%
IBU: 30–70
Glassware: pint,
nonic pint, snifter

This broad style has variety, but it all started with the intention to get good beer to people who were far away.

TROPICAL VOYAGER

Another stout with just enough differences from the base to qualify as a style. Originally, foreign stout was brewed stronger and hoppier in order to withstand the voyage to the more tropical parts of the British Empire. The style is typified by bittersweet roastiness and smooth darkness, but it can vary from there. Some are sweet and fruity, while others lean more bitter and dry. Even within the style there are subsets: tropical versions evoke sweeter notes of almost a rum quality, and exports tend to focus on bitterness and roasted malt. Generally both of these sub-styles show signs of coffee, bitter chocolate, and no hop flavor.

Three Beers to Try

GUINNESS FOREIGN EXTRA STOUT
Pours a deep black with a well-suited tan head. Full-bodied roastiness blends with layers of dark fruit, caramel, and dark bitter chocolate. Smooth and a must-try for the style.

LION STOUT   Malty and sweet, with hidden layers of fruit, caramel, and chocolate. Smooth mouthfeel with a bitter chocolate finish.

COOPERS BEST EXTRA STOUT   Drinkable
and full-bodied. Roasted malts on the nose and palate are mixed with coffee, light vanilla, and a balancing hop bitterness.

- Dark chocolate
- Bittersweet
- The precursor to this beer was called West Indies porter, and was brewed by Guinness in 1801.
- Beers in this style may be dry and bitter or sweet with fruit notes.
- Coffee
- The Pike Brewing Company
- Roasty
- Can be brewed with *Brettanomyces* yeast.
- Coopers Brewery
- Fs
- Guinness Foreign Extra Stout, the standard for the style, has been brewed since the early 1800s.
- Guinness & Co.
- Lion Brewery (Ceylon)
- Also known as tropical stouts.
- Desnoes & Geddes

Food Pairing

Oysters	Dark chocolate	Smoked or grilled meats

Imperial Russian Stout

Origin: England
Color: 30–40+ SRM
ABV: 7–13%
IBU: 50–90
Glassware: snifter

It's no wonder the Russian tsars of the 1700s loved this brew. Hugely roasty, it coats as you sip—practically a liquid dessert.

A HUGE BEER

In many ways, imperial Russian stouts are the biggest of beers. Consistently high in alcohol content, they hide it well between a massive malt bill and flavors that range from soft vanilla to dark chocolate and bitter coffee. The mouthfeel is coating, thick, and rich, and the color an opaque black. There is a prevalent forward roastiness that provides the foundation on which each brewer's unique creation is built. A huge beer, and if you're bold enough—or simply intrigued—there is a wealth of amazing beers in this category to try.

Three Beers to Try

COURAGE IMPERIAL RUSSIAN STOUT
The original imperial exported to Catherine II of Russia. Revived in 2011 by Wells & Young's, it boasts a smooth mouthfeel mingled with rich espresso notes, fruit, and a dark chocolate finish.

LE COQ IMPERIAL EXTRA DOUBLE STOUT   A balance of hops and malt, this beer, brewed by Harveys, leans on a heavy fruitiness.

OLD RASPUTIN RUSSIAN IMPERIAL STOUT   Brewed by North Coast, this brew has become the go-to imperial stout for many enthusiasts.

Imperial Russian Stout

Ims

- Barrel-aged versions are quite popular.
- Stone Brewing Co.
- Founders Brewing Co.
- Pairs surprisingly well with desserts.
- Rich
- Viscous
- Courage Russian Imperial Stout is said to be drinkable—even improved—after up to 13 years of aging.
- Wells & Young's Brewing Company
- Harvey & Son
- This imperial stout is called "Russian imperial" to acknowledge its appeal to the Russian court of the 18th century.
- North Coast Brewing Company
- Malty
- Roasty
- This style has bred a cult following with fans willing to wait hours for special one-time releases.
- Chocolaty
- Mikkeller

Food Pairing

Chocolate	Crème brûlée	Ice cream	Fruit tarts

ALES OF CONTINENTAL EUROPEAN ORIGIN

ALES OF CONTINENTAL EUROPEAN ORIGIN

Beyond the United Kingdom and Ireland, the birthplace of most European beers is primarily from one of two dominating countries on the Continent. As different in beer styles as two nations could be, Germany and Belgium have historically garnered the strongest influence on the Continental brewing scene. Belgium, with its ever-influential yeast, a mazed myriad of nuance and complexity, continues to defy style groups and rigid classifications, while maintaining excellence in product and beer culture. Germany, on the other hand, with roots in the *Reinheitsgebot* brewing purity laws, continues to produce an impressive stable of ales, most still strictly adhering to traditional styles and brewing guidelines.

Belgium has passionately embraced beer through the ages, and that historic devotion and attention to excellence still seeps through in both the brewing and the drinking culture. Most Belgian beers have a particular style of serving glass and many cafés, anchored deeply in rich traditions, forbid the serving of beer in any glass but its intended. The Belgian brewer is considered a creative— an artist continually perfecting his craft—and it is the drinker's pleasure to imbibe their delicious work.

In Belgian beer, yeast is the prominent player. Where a taste for bold and brash may be yearned for elsewhere in the world, the complex, nuanced, and intricate aromas and flavors of Belgian beer is what garners the attention of the drinker willing to take the first adventurous sip. It is a journey that few will regret. Many Belgian ales come packed with a sleeping alcoholic punch that hides coyly beneath the array of intriguing flavors. Most beers, when paired correctly with food, create a memorable culinary experience.

Trappist ales are brewed on a monastery property and under direction of the monks that live there. The term, "Trappiste," is an appellation and legally protects eight breweries—Achel, Chimay, La Trappe/ Koningshoeven, Orval, Rochefort, Westmalle, Westvleteren, and Stift Engelszell. All are held in justifiably high regard, each excellent, and many of the beers produced mark the apex of their style. While other secular brewers have crafted similar styles, they cannot bear the Trappiste title, and are instead dubbed Abbey ales. These too are not to be overlooked— many rival their sacred counterparts.

With some of the greatest and longest-standing beer traditions in the world, Germany continues to produce brews that are the standard for their style. While pale lagers have stolen the spotlight of modern-day brewing in Germany, until the 16th century the nation only produced ales.

Wheat beers—Weissbiers—dominate German ales, ranging from the light, tart, and spritzy Berliner Weisse all the way to the rich and warming Weizenbock. The differentiating ingredient, wheat, is the stitch that runs through this patchwork quilt of styles and flavors, yet the variance between each type is surprising, as some seem to have entirely unrelated palate profiles.

Alongside Germany's famous lagers and ales, two sister styles, Kölsch and Altbier, are the oddities—hybrids that each undergo warm fermentation followed by a period of the cold conditioning usually associated with lagers. Two beers closely connected with the cities from which they come, the ancient Altbier maintains a stronghold in its hometown of Düsseldorf, while Kölsch, Altbier's pale sister, was born in Köln.

Witbier

Origin: Belgium
Color: 2-4 SRM
ABV: 4.5-5.5%
IBU: 10-20
Glassware: pint, mug

Crisp, effervescent, and zesty this beer went from obscurity in the 1950s to become a style brewed and enjoyed worldwide.

A WHITER SHADE OF PALE

To the French, it's "bière blanche;" to the Belgians, it's "witbier;" to the Japanese, it's "white ale," but to beer lovers worldwide, it's just plain good. A straw-yellow beer with a steady, billowing cap of white foam that leaves cascading sheets of lace, this brew transcends geographical barriers with its notable blend of spices and its slightly acidic, slightly sour flavor. The nose is a blend of dirty lemon and yeast, with a complex combination of cleansing bubbles and smooth mouthfeel. The finish is dry and refreshing. It's a brew full of contradictions and oddly pleasing combinations. A complexity worth simply enjoying.

Three Beers to Try

HOEGAARDEN WIT   The beer with which brewer Pierre Celis revived the long-lost style in 1966.

ALLAGASH WHITE   The Maine brewery's style is spiced with the usual suspects: coriander and Curaçao orange.

UNIBROUE BLANCHE DE CHAMBLY
This Canadian take on witbier was the first of its kind in North America,

Tart

Brouwerij Bavik

Allagash Brewing Company

Named for its cloudiness and pale color, it is called "bière blanche" in France, "witbier" in Belgium, and "white ale" in other parts of the world.

In 1966, at what was then called Brouwerij Celis in Hoegaarden, Belgium, Pierre Celis revived the style.

Kiuchi Brewery

Wit

Hoegaarden

Brouwerij St. Bernadus

Effervescent

Spicy

Unibroue

Blue Moon brewery's Belgian White is a best-selling example of the style and has been a gateway beer for many into the craft beer world.

By 1955 the style had gone all but extinct.

Zesty

Citrus

Food Pairing

| Salmon | Poultry | Goat cheese | Apple pie |

Gose

Origin: Germany
Color: 2-4 SRM
ABV: 4.5-5.5%
IBU: 4-9
Glassware: stange

A rarity in the beer world, and a difficult beer to find, Gose has intriguing and unique qualities only found in this style.

THE SALTED DEEP

In the beer world there are palate-punishing hop bombs, motor-oil thick stouts, and taste-bud assaulting sour beers. Gose is none of these. Hidden behind a veil of murky gold are dancing bubbles, lightening the mouthfeel to medium, and making the sour bite refreshingly so. Gose is sour, but not mouth-puckering, and it finishes clean and dry. There can be fruity complexities with green apple notes and hints of banana, often with a reasonably prominent spicing of coriander. An oddity unique to this style, Gose is brewed with salt, adding depth to the mouthfeel and body rather than any specific flavor.

Three Beers to Try

LEIPZIGER GOSE   From the Bayerischer Bahnhof, this is the classic and most common example of the style. A complex blend of fruit. Finishes dry with a slight hint of salt.

VERLOREN   This beer from the Boston Beer Company pours a hazy deep gold with an up-front nose of coriander and fruit. These aromas continue on the palate on a foundation of smooth fruit and slight saltiness.

UPRIGHT BREWING COMPANY GOSE
A dry finish preceded by a smooth body. Slight notes of lemon mix with a tactful tartness. A traditional take on the style.

THE ATOMIC STRUCTURE OF
Gose

Gs

Sour

Fruity

Brauhaus Goslar

After an almost 40-year absence, Gose began to be brewed again following the fall of the Berlin Wall.

goz-uh

Pronounced *goz-uh.*

Upright Brewing Company

Salt is added to the water used in the brewing process.

Bayerischer Bahnhof

Dry

Due to its use of salt, Gose does not meet the standards of the *Reinheitsgebot* (Bavarian Beer Purity Law) used in brewing. However, it is granted an exception as a specialty of its home region.

Named after Goslar, the town in which Gose was originally popular.

The Boston Beer Company

Puckering

Cascade Brewing

Crisp

Food Pairing

| Strong seafood | Light Thai food | Salmon salad |

Berliner Weisse

**Origin: Berlin,
Germany
Color: 2–4 SRM
ABV: 2.5–3.5%
IBU: 3–8
Glassware: chalice**

When it's time to toast, this brew can do the job. Bubbly, refreshing, and mouth-puckering, it shows just how vast the boundaries of beer are.

BRING OUT THE FRUIT

Napoleon declared Berliner Weisse the champagne of beers. Sprightly, bubbly, and acidic to the point of sour, this brew from Berlin has been traditionally tempered by fruit syrups—almost an adult kiddie cocktail. One of the few places where a post-brew additive is acceptable, a Berliner Weisse can be almost too much pucker without a bit of sweet fruitiness to tone it down. Raspberry syrup and herbal essence of woodruff are the most frequently chosen additives. The body is hazy, highly carbonated, and capped with a white, airy head. It smells of yeast and hay with a slight, pleasant funkiness.

Three Beers to Try

BAYERISCHER BAHNHOF BERLINER STYLE WEISSE   Less sharp and acidic than the classic beer of the style. Still tart, but more mellow.

PROFESSOR FRITZ BRIEM 1809 BERLINER WEISSE   Created by Professor Fritz Briem in an attempt to revive this once almost extinct style.

BERLINER KINDL WEISSE   Even for the style, this version of Berliner Weisse has an intense, acidic sourness

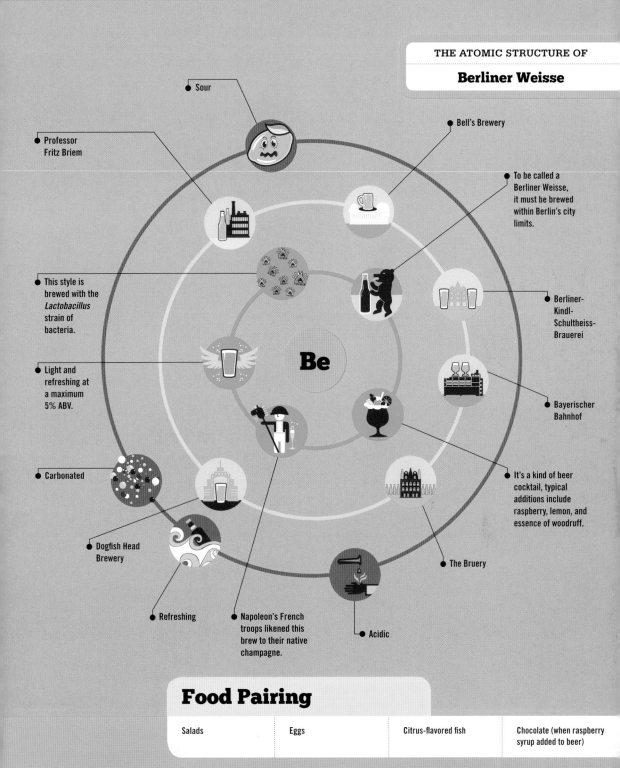

- Sour
- Professor Fritz Briem
- Bell's Brewery
- To be called a Berliner Weisse, it must be brewed within Berlin's city limits.
- This style is brewed with the *Lactobacillus* strain of bacteria.
- Berliner-Kindl-Schultheiss-Brauerei
- Light and refreshing at a maximum 5% ABV.
- Bayerischer Bahnhof
- Carbonated
- It's a kind of beer cocktail, typical additions include raspberry, lemon, and essence of woodruff.
- Dogfish Head Brewery
- The Bruery
- Refreshing
- Napoleon's French troops likened this brew to their native champagne.
- Acidic

Be

Food Pairing

| Salads | Eggs | Citrus-flavored fish | Chocolate (when raspberry syrup added to beer) |

Kölsch

Origin: Germany
Color: 3.5–5 SRM
ABV: 4.4–5.2%
IBU: 20–30
Glassware: stange

A delicious crossbreed, this ale has all the characteristics of a light, quenching lager.

EFFERVESCENT AND BRILLIANTLY CLEAR

Indigenous to Köln (Cologne), Germany, Kölsch is a top-fermented, cold-conditioned hybrid. Features of both ale and lager come through: a slight ale fruitiness dances through the straw-blonde body with the clean, crisp, delicacy of a lager. A soft maltiness caresses, giving an utterly smooth and refreshing character. With origins in its sister style, Altbier (see page 108), it is a young brew, its modern rendition introduced as recently as 1918. It is effervescent and brilliantly clear, and is one of the styles behind which there is little for a brewer's mistakes to hide. Its mild flavor can contain notes of bread, fruit, hops, and cereal grains.

Three Beers to Try

REISSDORF KÖLSCH   A biscuity, malty nose mixes with pleasant citrus and floral notes. It is gently carbonated and very refreshing and crisp.

SÜNNER KÖLSCH   The brewery responsible for designating the style "Kölsch," created this classic. Bread and apples on the nose, floral hops play through a clean body.

GAFFEL KÖLSCH   Highly effervescent, it has distinct notes of pepper strewn about a sweet maltiness. A clean finish with

Fruity

Biscuity

Clean

Metropolitan Brewing

True Kölsch is served in Köln, by *Kobes*, waiters wearing a uniform of blue shirt and leather apron.

Typically brewed solely with pale Pilsner malt.

Privatbrauerei Gaffel Becker & Co.

Kol

This style is Germany's only real pale ale (made completely from barley).

The Boston Beer Company

The Kölsch Convention of 1986 ruled that only brewers located in Köln may legally call beer Kölsch. Outside of the city, producers describe their beer as "Kölsch-style."

Balanced

Sünner Brauerei

Privat-Brauerei Heinrich Reissdorf

Refreshing

Kölsch also means "Cologne-ish" and is the name for the region's local dialect.

Goose Island Beer Co.

Food Pairing

Salads	Light pork dishes	Eggs

Belgian Strong Pale Ale

Origin: Belgium
Color: 3.5–5.5 SRM
ABV: 7–9%
IBU: 25–45
Glassware: tulip, snifter, oversized wine glass

The classic beers of this style are highly alcoholic but fresh, zippy, refreshing, and spicy pale ales.

THE DEVIL INCARNATE

Built on a foundation laid by Brouwerij Duvel Moortgat, those brewing this style (also called strong golden or strong blonde) have traditionally been in competition to create a beer that compares to Duvel. Enticing and deceiving in pale yellow, beers of this type are dressed with an innocent linen-white cap that leaves stripes of streaked lace. Underneath this golden guise broods an intense alcohol. It is layered with fruits and spices to create a complex, crisp, and enjoyable blend. This mischievous deceiver has conjured up names deserving of its ploy: Duvel (devil), Damnation, and Lucifer to name a few.

Three Beers to Try

DUVEL   The absolute pinnacle of the style, this "devil" hides a powerful 8.5% ABV in a deceptively picture-perfect bright, clear, golden body and a billowing white head.

DELIRIUM TREMENS   Beads stream upward to create a pillowy head. Aroma of bright citrus, yeast, and hops. Brewed by Brouwerij Huyghe.

LA CHOUFFE   With a profound yeasty profile, this brew made by Achouffe toes the style line, with notes of tropical fruits and moderately bitter hops.

Unibroue

Clean

Brouwerij De Dolle Brouwers

Duvel was originally dark in color.

The creation of this style was, in part, initiated by the vogue for light pilsners.

Russian River Brewing Company

Spa

Effervescent

Brasserie d'Achouffe

Brouwerij Duvel Moortgat

The line between tripels and Belgian strong golden ales is blurry. If you like one, try the other.

Drinkable

With freshness and snappy carbonation, it makes a great aperitif.

Brouwerij Huyghe

Bitter

Food Pairing

Indian food	Pesto dishes	Chinese food	Shrimp

Bière de Champagne

Origin: Belgium
Color: 3-6 SRM
ABV: 9-14%
IBU: 10-30
Glassware: flute

A different take on the time-honored champagne toast, this beer may just begin a new tradition.

RAISE YOUR GLASS

This contemporary-style, effervescent, and toast-worthy beer has as intricate a process of production as champagne. It goes through a lengthy period of maturation and is then riddled (stored upside down and rotated) and disgorged (the settled yeast in the neck is removed), in the same manner as for sparkling wines. The result is a highly carbonated, refreshing, sparkling beer that is high in ABV. A refined selection, it is a beautiful accompaniment to light seafood or a delightful stand-alone drink before dinner.

Three Beers to Try

DEUS This beer by Brouwerij Bosteels has a beautiful golden body with an airy head. Its bright, fruity nose, full of citrus and herbs, is complemented by a smooth, but freshly bubbled feel.

INFINIUM A collaborative brew from the Boston Beer Company and Weihenstephan brewery. A stream of carbonation aids a light head. The aroma of bread and citric and ever-so-slight bitterness ends dry.

MALHEUR BRUT RESERVE Veiling the 12% ABV dangerously well, this beer is the lightest of straw in color and has a cap of white foam. Spicy, earthy, and tart on the nose, the alcohol surfaces on the sip, but melds into citrus and a malty, but dry finish.

A beer alternative to a champagne toast.

Mikkeller

A relatively new style, very few brewers do it well.

Brouwerij Malheur

Brouwerij Bosteels

Also called bière brut.

Ch

Effervescent

Cervejaria Sudbrack

Refined

Riddling and disgorgement, both champagne-making methods, are used in creating this beer.

The Boston Beer Company (in collaboration with Bayerische Staatsbrauerei Weihenstephan)

Produced most frequently today in France and Belgium.

Light

Dry

Citrus

Food pairing

Shellfish	Fish	Berries

Kristalweizen

Origin: Germany
Color: 2–8 SRM
ABV: 4–5.5%
IBU: 10–15
Glassware: weizen

A filtered version of Weissbier (page 86), this beer is a body of refreshing complexities that suits many foods and many moods.

CLEAN AND CLEAR

In a sector of beer where cloudy styles reign supreme, this brew sticks out like a teenager with something to prove. The body of a Kristalweizen is like gold-tinted glass, busy with cascading carbonation. Almost visible notes of banana, clove, and bubble gum waft out of the puffy white head, which streaks a delicate lace. It's clean and refreshing without weakness in its mouthfeel. While maintaining the classic versatility of the characteristic wheat-beer style, the filtered, clear flair of Kristalweizen makes it a very palatable transition from less interesting, light beers.

Three Beers to Try

WEIHENSTEPHANER KRISTALLWEISSBIER   As near a perfect example of the style as you will find. Refreshing, fruity, clean.

ERDINGER WEISSBRAU WEISSBIER KRISTALLKLAR   Clean and clear, medium-bodied with a touch of spice, this beer is made by a significant Weissbier brewery.

BRAUEREI TUCHER BRAU KRISTALL WEIZEN   Light and highly effervescent with a slight, pleasant tang.

THE ATOMIC STRUCTURE OF
Kristalweizen

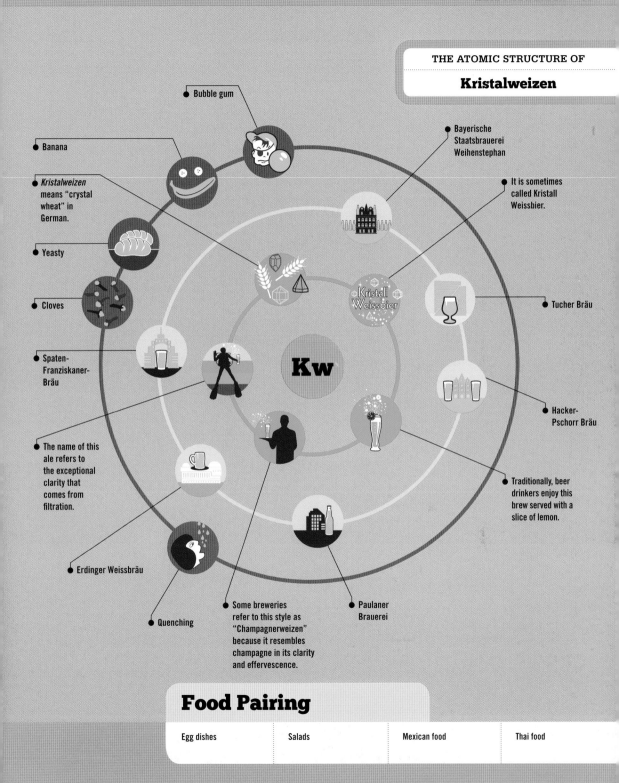

- Bubble gum
- Banana
- *Kristalweizen* means "crystal wheat" in German.
- Yeasty
- Cloves
- Spaten-Franziskaner-Bräu
- The name of this ale refers to the exceptional clarity that comes from filtration.
- Erdinger Weissbräu
- Quenching
- Some breweries refer to this style as "Champagnerweizen" because it resembles champagne in its clarity and effervescence.
- Paulaner Brauerei
- Bayerische Staatsbrauerei Weihenstephan
- It is sometimes called Kristall Weissbier.
- Tucher Bräu
- Hacker-Pschorr Bräu
- Traditionally, beer drinkers enjoy this brew served with a slice of lemon.

Kristall Weissbier

Kw

Food Pairing

| Egg dishes | Salads | Mexican food | Thai food |

Weissbier

Origin: Germany
Color: 2-9 SRM
ABV: 4-5.5%
IBU: 10-18
Glassware: weizen

Incredibly versatile, Weissbier—the classic wheat beer—is a wonderfully satisfying brew that befits many occasions.

THE FATHER OF WHEAT BEERS

In a world where the slightest nuance signals the birth of an entirely new category of beer, Weissbier is the standard from which many new categories are born. A clear Weissbier becomes a Kristalweizen, a dark one becomes a Dunkelweizen. This father of wheat beers is a surprising contrast of pure, clear refreshment, from a hazy, unfiltered, bubbling body of orange, with a tall crown of a head sitting majestically atop. The nose and flavor are typically a pleasant mix of yeast, citrus, banana, and clove. There is a power in versatility, as Weissbier can be the perfect accompaniment to many a meal. From egg dishes to spicy pad thai to homemade apple pie, this beer stands up to them all—but it's also perfect for drinking on its own.

Three Beers to Try

WEIHENSTEPHANER HEFEWEISSBIER
One of the great examples of the style, well-built in body, complex in aroma and spice—a standard for comparison.

PAULANER HEFE-WEISSBIER NATURTRÜB Beautiful body of orange and a delicately balanced blend of yeast, fruit, and spice.

ERDINGER WEISSBIER The king of the wide range of beers produced by Erdinger, this bottle-conditioned beer is ready to drink after just 3–4 weeks in the bottle.

THE ATOMIC STRUCTURE OF

Weissbier

Wb

Banana

Bubble gum

Yeasty

Bayerische Staatsbrauerei Weihenstephan

Cloves

Erdinger Weissbräu

This style is also known as Hefeweizen, Weizenbier, and wheat ale.

Spaten-Franziskaner-Bräu

Paulaner Brauerei

In 2013 there were more than 1,000 Weissbier brands on the market.

German law stipulates that a beer true to this style must be brewed with at least 50% malted wheat.

Brauerei Aying

Quenching

The glass for Weissbier is a tall, curved, tulip shape and the proper pour is almost a ritual.

Hacker-Pschorr Bräu

Food Pairing

| Egg dishes | Salads | Mexican food | Thai food | German food |

Tripel

Origin: Belgium
Color: 3.5–7 SRM
ABV: 7.5–9.5%
IBU: 20–40
Glassware: tulip, goblet

The delicately complex and surprisingly spirituous tripel is a young style that has been beautifully matured.

A GLASS OF SUNSHINE

Pouring into the glass like sunshine, its golden-yellow haze is mesmerizing and the cotton-white, bulbous head literally climbs the glass to the rim. Through the thick foam rises a medley of spices, malt, and yeast. The palate is complex and sweet, but can be slightly bitter. The texture feels soft and delicate. Tripel's yeast characteristics are a focal point, often a potpourri: cinnamon, clove, pepper, banana, tangerines, lemon, orange, apple, and peach. Another Belgian deviant in disguise, the tripel style can be potent, yet amazingly drinkable.

Three Beers to Try

WESTMALLE TRIPEL   The benchmark for the style, this beer is bright golden with a billowing white head. It has a nose of citrus fruits, cloves, and hops and a crisp, light, cleansing mouthfeel.

LA FIN DU MONDE   By Unibroue, this beer is golden-orange with a white crown. Smooth and creamy, it has a complex blend of spices and an underlying sweetness that finishes just bitter enough.

TRIPEL KARMELIET   Family-owned for seven generations, Brouwerij Bosteels makes a fine tripel. A bursting bouquet of citrus, earth, and spice meld together in a caramel-sweet body that coats before a clean finish.

THE ATOMIC STRUCTURE OF

Tripel

The only true "Trappist" tripels are those brewed at Trappist monasteries. They are Chimay, La Trappe, Achel, and Westmalle.

Bières de Chimay

Yeasty

First produced in 1934, Westmalle Tripel was the first of its kind.

Tripels not brewed at Trappist monasteries are classified as Abbey-style tripels.

Brouwerij St. Bernardus

Unibroue

Tr

Brouwerij Bosteels

Delicate

It is not known for certain where this style got its name. Some believe it refers to the number of fermentations, some to the alcohol content.

Bierbrouwerij De Koningshoeven

Complex

Spicy

Brewing scientist, Henrik Verlinden, was the only non-Trappist brewer allowed to sell his beer as a Trappist style.

Brouwerij der Trappisten van Westmalle

Food Pairing

| Basil-flavored foods | Grilled salmon | Asparagus | Lobster |

Belgian Pale Ale

Origin: Belgium
Color: 4–14 SRM
ABV: 3.9–5.6%
IBU: 20–30
Glassware: snifter, tulip, oversized wine glass

The melting pot of beers that are amber in color and with a notable hoppiness, Belgian brews that fit in this style feature a complexity in yeast and malts that set them apart.

SHADES OF BRONZE

Belgians—brewers and drinkers alike—rarely categorize their domestic beer. Each beer has been crafted in a way that deserves its own place in the beer world. However, there is a class of ales that have the look and feel of pale ale brewed elsewhere and so have been grouped as such.

A Belgian pale (also called golden or blonde) is typically a light bronze to a deeper copper in color. Generally clear, it is focused less on a bitter hopping than on the complexities shown in both the yeast and the malts. Medium in body and smooth, they are highly drinkable and with hints of light fruit, oranges, spices, cinnamon, and an intriguing maltiness.

Three Beers to Try

DE KONINCK   When in Antwerp, any barkeeper knows what you want when you say a "*bolleke*"—this beer. Biscuity, fruity aromas from a deep amber body. Chewy texture of fruit and yeasty in taste.

RARE VOS   Named after the Brussels pub and meaning "sly fox," it is deep amber, with a brilliant Belgian nose of orange, spices, and caramel. Made by Ommegang.

REDEMPTION   This Russian River brew pours a hazy apricot with a white whipped head. The smell is a pleasing combination of yeasty farmhouse funk and light fruit that becomes a drinkable spiciness on first sip.

THE ATOMIC STRUCTURE OF
Belgian Pale Ale

Despite its 300 year history, today's exemplars of the style were perfected in just the past 70 years.

Subtle fruit

Yeasty

Huisbrouwerij De Halve Maan

At many traditional Belgian cafés, if the proper glassware is not available, they will not serve the beer.

Russian River Brewing Company

Soft maltiness

New Belgium Brewing Company

Bpa

Also called blonde and golden.

Brewery Ommegang

The early examples of the style arose from the desire for lighter beer around the world in the 1700s.

Brouwerij De Koninck

The proper pour for this beer, and most Belgians brews, should leave the remaining sediment in the bottle.

Leffe (InBev Belgium)

Spicy

Food Pairing

Pork	Fried fish	Sausages	Thai food	Salads

Lambic

Origin: Belgium
Color: 3-7 SRM
ABV: 5-6%
IBU: 0-10
**Glassware: flute,
oversized wine
glass**

The lambic family is made up of three distinct sub-styles: unblended lambic, gueuze, and fruit lambic. The first is the base for the others and is quite uncommon outside of Brussels.

CHARACTERFUL BACTERIA

While lambics of old are becoming increasingly rare, those still being brewed are complex and intriguing. Unblended lambics can be both young and old, depending on the amount of time spent in the barrel. Young brews are more lively and carbonated, perhaps with a slightly more puckering tartness. Mature lambics have a mellow smoothness and more of the complexities that come with the bacteria involved in the brewing process. These bacteria, intentional and desirable, give an unparalleled depth of character. It becomes pleasantly musty, lending a barnyard, leathery aroma and taste. The style is typically served from the cask and is very dry with little carbonation.

Three Beers to Try

CANTILLON BRUOCSELLA GRAND CRU
Aged on oak for three years, a funky, intense nose of earth results. It is textured and complex.

CANTILLON IRIS   Brewed to celebrate the 20th anniversary of the Brussels Museum of Gueuze, it is amber and more bitter than some lambics due to the use of fresh hops.

OUDE LAMBIEK DE CAM   A musty nose of wet hay and slight fruity notes gathers in complexity and intensity on the palate

THE ATOMIC STRUCTURE OF

Lambic

L

Sour

Brouwerij Lindemans

Lambic is probably named after the small Belgian town of Lembeek.

Fruity

Oaky

Best known in Brussels, Belgium.

Brouwerij Boon

Almost identical to lambics brewed in the 1600s.

Intense

Only brewed between October and May, when the climate is ideal for the growth of the necessary microorganisms.

Brasserie Cantillon Brouwerij

De Cam Geuzestekerij

Complex

Brouwerij Girardin

Traditionally, lambics are fermented in open air, allowing spontaneous fermentation by wild yeast strains.

Food Pairing

| Stews | Fish | Sauerkraut |

Gueuze

Origin: Belgium
Color: 3–13 SRM
ABV: 5–8%
IBU: 0–23
Glassware: flute

A blend of young and old lambic, gueuze is tempered but still tart, sour, and involved.

BLENDED TO PERFECTION

Easier to find than unblended lambic, gueuze still bears the notable lambic complexities and characteristics. Typically three, but up to as many as seven, lambics are blended to create the brewer's perfect rendering. After the process of artistic blending, the gueuze is bottled and aged again, typically for three to nine months, but sometimes longer. The result is highly effervescent and refreshing.

Three Beers to Try

CANTILLON GUEUZE 100% LAMBIC   Pours a burnt orange with a thick lace. The musty, barnyard scent blends with lemon and oak. This beer accounts for half of Cantillon's entire production.

GUEUZE CUVÉE RENÉ   A nose of utter complexity characterizes this brew by Lindemans. Sweetness of honey mixes with sour fruit and a barnyard aroma. Refreshingly tart from beginning to end.

OUD BEERSEL OUDE GEUZE VIEILLE   Brewed in Beersel, this is a traditional offering from the brewer. Pouring golden amber, it is smooth and sour with a refreshing bitterness. A contradiction and a delight.

Sour

Sweet

Brouwerij Oud Beersel

Fruity

Pronounced with a hard "g" and rhymes with "cursor"—*gerz-uh.*

Nuanced

GERZ-UH

Brouwerij Boon

Sometimes called "Brussels champagne."

G

Traditionally bottled with a cork and wire cap.

Brouwerij Lindemans

1875
1850

The word "gueuze" may come from the same root as gas, ghost, geyser, or the Flemish word *gist,* which means "yeast."

Brasserie Cantillon Brouwerij

Hanssens Artisanaal

Complex

Gueuze was created between 1850 and 1875.

Brouwerij Girardin

Food Pairing

| Serve as an aperitif | Mussels | Oysters | Goat cheese |

Fruit Lambic

Origin: Belgium
Color: 3–7 SRM
(varies with fruit)
ABV: 5–7%
IBU: 0–10
Glassware: flute

A beer that's hard to believe it's a beer, this style has a punch of fruit to balance the tartness.

A REFRESHING DESSERT DRINK

Much of the basic lambic story is the same here as for gueuze (see page 94). The base beer, before fruit is added, is typically a blend of young and old lambics. Once the brewer has found that perfect marriage of the two, fruit is added and the secondary fermentation begins. The specific fruit used is up to the brewer, but the most common are cherries, raspberries, black currants, apples, and peaches. The result is a product of the specific fruit addition, but will be a complex mélange of tart, fruity, dry, effervescent, and crisp. This style is refreshing and can be delicious paired with dessert or served alone.

Three Beers to Try

KRIEK BOON   A brilliantly red body and a light pink head, the nose is all cherry. The tartness continues on the palate, balanced by just enough sweetness.

ROSÉ DE GAMBRINUS   A framboise made by Cantillon, one of the world's great crafters of lambic. A beautiful deep pink with up-front tartness and well-rounded fruit.

LINDEMANS PÊCHE   The nose is immediately peaches, the palate is tangy peach with a hint of earthiness.

THE ATOMIC STRUCTURE OF

Fruit Lambic

Fruity

Tart

Brouwerij Timmermans

In order to increase the selection available to its patrons, Belgian cafés began adding fruit to their lambics.

Brewing of lambic dates back to as early as the mid-1500s.

1500's

Upland Brewing Company

Hanssens Artisanaal

The first fruits used in lambics were sour cherries.

Brouwerij Lindemans

Some fruit lambics are fermented with fruit and some with fruit juices.

The fruits most often used are: cherry (*kriek*), raspberry (*framboise*), blackcurrant (*cassis*), and peach (*pêche*).

Brasserie Cantillon Brouwerij

Crisp

Dry

Brouwerij Boon

Lf

Food Pairing

| Chocolate desserts | Cheesecake | Sweet cheeses |

Belgian IPA

Origin: Belgium
Color: 3-19 SRM
ABV: 6-10.5%
IBU: 50-80
Glassware: tulip

The beauty of beer is that it is ever changing. This style, new to the craft brewing scene, is one such tasty example.

BELGIAN YEAST AND HOPS

With the rise in popularity of IPAs worldwide, Belgian brewers, who traditionally had not produced hop-forward beer, began to experiment. The blend of the famed Belgian yeast strains with a hop-heavy palate was a dream match. From the outset it is impressive: a golden to amber body, hazy but brilliant, punctuated with a bright white cap. The nose continues the intrigue, an impossible blend of hops and earthy, biscuity, distinct yeast. Keeping the combination in a tightrope balance becomes the key—American brewers lean more on the hops, while Belgians tend to be more focused on the yeast. A developing style, it is worth doing your own research.

Three Beers to Try

HOUBLON CHOUFFE   Brewed in 2006 by Achouffe for the first time, it was a pioneer. Bright gold, puffy white head with an immediate hop punch. The Belgian influence leans toward tripel. An incredible combination.

STONE CALI-BELGIQUE   An American hop bill with citrus and floral notes, this golden-orange brew is bitter, but not overly so, and remains focused on the Belgian yeast character.

DE RANKE XX BITTER   A spicy, floral, hoppy nose emits from a body of hazy apricot. Big, bitter hops and a nicely spicy yeast strain are present throughout.

Brouwerij De Leyerth (Urthel)

Brouwerij Duvel Moortgat

Typically the hops used are American varieties.

Yeasty

Also referred to as "white IPA."

Deschutes Brewery

Bli

This is a new style that is still evolving.

Brouwerij De Ranke

Stone Brewing Co.

Floral

Ironically, the style is typically too hoppy for most Belgian beer drinkers.

Citric

Brasserie d'Achouffe

Many use authentic Trappist ale yeast.

Bitter

Food Pairing

| Fried chicken | Spicy seafood | Gorgonzola | Thai food |

Saison

Origin: Belgium
Color: 5-14 SRM
ABV: 4.5-8%
IBU: 20-45
Glassware: tulip

A style with seemingly limitless boundaries, saisons give the brewer freedom to create and the drinker freedom to enjoy.

A SUMMER BREW

While the characteristics of this style vary, the history is relatively consistent. Traditionally brewed in late winter or early spring, saison (meaning "season") beers, were meant to last the farmer-brewer from March to October. The summer months brought warm weather and difficult brewing conditions, so what was brewed in the spring was what would be consumed through the harvest.

The saison style is typically rustic and earthy, spicy, and peppery. It varies in color, but centers around a pale orange hue, with streaming carbonation and a buoyant vanilla head. Bright and refreshing, it finishes dry, with a pleasing and cleansing tart bite. Markedly bitter to survive the year, these beers are balanced enough to be perfectly quenching.

Three Beers to Try

SAISON DUPONT VIEILLE PROVISION
The flagship saison, this is one to be tried. A nose to die for, earthy, spicy with coriander, pepper, and a veritable fruit feast. Pale golden and hazy, it becomes bitter, earthy, slightly sweet, and wonderfully refreshing.

SAISON D'EREZÉE—PRINTEMPS Fantôme produces an array of saisons. This has lemon and hay aromas, and a light farmhouse funkiness. Light, refreshing, and hopped.

OMMEGANG HENNEPIN A brilliant hazy gold with citrus and spiced aromatics that carry through the palate. Sweetness blends and finishes refreshingly dry.

THE ATOMIC STRUCTURE OF

Saison

Brasserie Dupont

Saint Somewhere Brewing Company

Jolly Pumpkin Artisan Ales

Typically brewed by farmers as a refreshing drink for the harvest.

Also called farmhouse ales.

Brasserie Fantôme

Brewery Ommegang

Incredibly versatile food-pairing beer.

Hoppy

Brouwerij Duvel Moortgat

Peppery

S

Refreshing

Dry

Citrus

Spicy

Traditionally brewed in the province of Hainaut in Belgium's southern region of Wallonia.

Food Pairing

| Crab cakes | Sausages | Thai food | Aged Gouda |

Bière de Garde

Origin: France
Color: 6–19 SRM
ABV: 6–8.5%
IBU: 18–30
Glassware: tulip

The name of this farmhouse ale, which originated in northern France, means literally "beer for keeping."

A FREESTYLE BREW

This style can be formally divided into three sub-categories according to color: brown, blonde, and amber. However, these subdivisions are at odds with the philosophy of the style, which emphasizes artistic freedom and interpretation. Yet, a few lines must be drawn.

At its core is a soft maltiness, developed further by spiciness and mustiness and tactfully balanced by restrained hops. It checks in at 6–8.5 percent alcohol and finishes crisp and refreshing. A musty, earthy complexity sets it apart as a most intriguing beer.

Three Beers to Try

JENLAIN (AMBER) This beer by Duyck kept the style from the grave. A bronzed amber with a velvety cap. A soft palate of sweet malt ends with a crisp finish.

CH'TI BLONDE (Sold in the United States as Castelain.) Brewed by Brasserie Castelain, which uses lager yeast in their bières de garde. This well-balanced beer pours golden, with an earthy, slightly citric, and spiced nose.

LA BIÈRE DES SANS CULOTTES A lacy crown graces the deep gold body of this beer by La Choulette. Earthy notes on the nose and palate blend with spice and a refreshing hop bite.

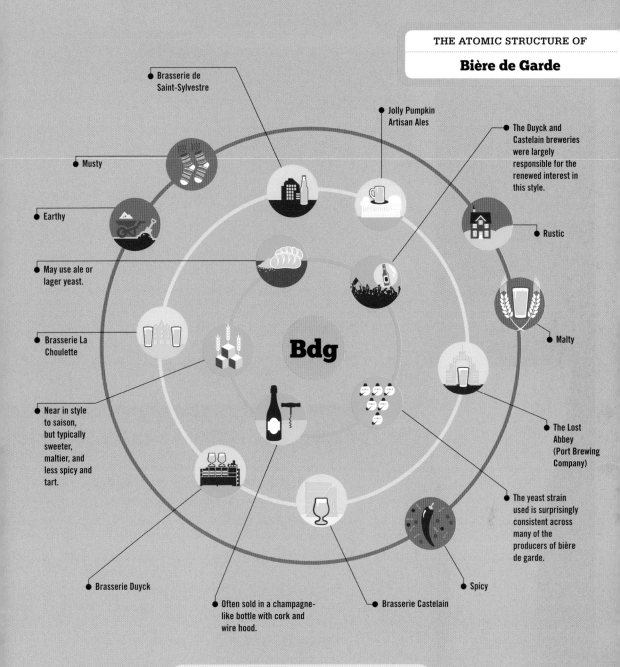

Brasserie de Saint-Sylvestre

Jolly Pumpkin Artisan Ales

The Duyck and Castelain breweries were largely responsible for the renewed interest in this style.

Musty

Earthy

Rustic

May use ale or lager yeast.

Malty

Brasserie La Choulette

Bdg

Near in style to saison, but typically sweeter, maltier, and less spicy and tart.

The Lost Abbey (Port Brewing Company)

The yeast strain used is surprisingly consistent across many of the producers of bière de garde.

Brasserie Duyck

Spicy

Often sold in a champagne-like bottle with cork and wire hood.

Brasserie Castelain

Food Pairing

| Pungent French cheese | Sausages | Lamb chops | Turkey |

Dunkelweizen

Origin: Germany
Color: 9-13 SRM
ABV: 4.5-6%
IBU: 10-18
Glassware: weizen

For a meatier version of Weissbier (page 86), Dunkelweizen hits the mark. Drinkable, refreshing, and complex, there are many world-class beers in this category.

DEEPER AND DARKER

The towering head that typifies the Weissbier is no less impressive in its darker brother. Dunkelweizen's head is off-white and sponge-like; the body is a hazy, caramelly orange, with the signature carbonation streaking up the glass. The depth follows through on the nose, with just a slightly heavier undercurrent of wheat, malt, and roastiness. There can be light notes of chocolate and fruit woven through a varied spiciness. Typically the mouthfeel is creamy and smooth, and the finish refreshingly crisp. With its richness and body, Dunkelweizen is a great choice as a cool-weather alternative to the more summery Weissbier.

Three Beers to Try

WEIHENSTEPHANER HEFEWEISSBIER DUNKEL Silky smooth without being cloying. Surprisingly refreshing with complex flavors.

AYINGER UR-WEISSE Malty nose and body with a cohesive blend of fruit, spice, and malt. Creamy and rich.

FRANZISKANER HEFE-WEISSE DUNKEL Sweet and quite malty with a coating texture. Fruity and medium-bodied, it has a dry finish.

Dunkelweizen

Dk

- Fruity
- Caramelly
- Bayerische Staatsbrauerei Weihenstephan
- Brauerei Aying
- *Dunkel* means "dark" in German.
- Roasty
- Dunkelweizen is a darker version of Weissbier (page 86).
- Caramelized and roasted malts provide color and flavor.
- Gordon Biersch Brewing Company
- Creamy
- The Vienna and/or Munich malts give the Dunkelweizen its deep color and rich taste.
- Hacker-Pschorr Bräu
- Smooth
- Paulaner Brauerei
- Evidence found in 1935 suggests that dark wheat beer was made in Germany as early as 800 BCE.
- Spaten-Franziskaner-Bräu

Food Pairing

German food	Sausages	Enchiladas	Pulled pork

Flanders Red

Origin: Belgium
Color: 10-16 SRM
ABV: 4.5-6.5%
IBU: 10-25
Glassware: flute, tulip

A deceptive pour of soft garnet and brown, this beer is not for the faint of heart.

FUNKY FARMYARD FAVORITE

Flanders red ale has its origins in the westernmost parts of Belgium. Unsurprisingly, it pours a deep reddish brown. It is intense in tartness and satisfying complexity. Typically the immediate impacts are earthiness, unusual yeasts, and an intriguing balance of sweet and sour, but some can have hints of vanilla, oak, wet wool, lemons, sherry, and cherries. It is normally the product of young and old blends and is aged for up to three years in unlined oak vats. During aging, wild yeast strains come to the fore, creating a barnyard funk that melds with sweet and fruity malt flavors. A bold style that, with an open mind, can become a favorite.

Three Beers to Try

RODENBACH GRAND CRU From the most famous producer of the style, this beer has an almost-brown body with a citrusy, earthy, funky nose. Malty, but tart and refreshing.

DUCHESSE DE BOURGOGNE Red with bronze lowlights and a bountiful head. The barnyard scent mixes with sour fruit and malt. The sour is tempered somewhat by earthiness, but is wonderfully balanced. From Verhaeghe.

CUVÉE DES JACOBINS ROUGE Family-owned since 1892, the Brouwerij Bockor produces this brilliantly balanced

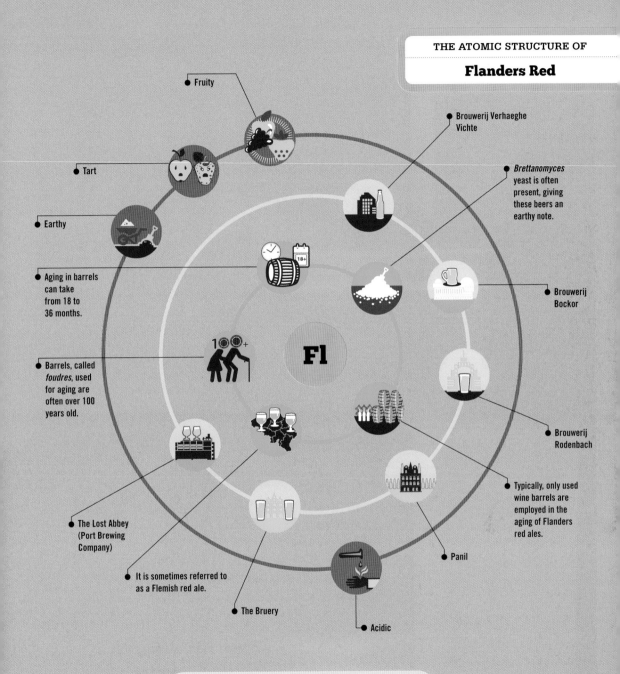

Fruity

Tart

Earthy

Brouwerij Verhaeghe Vichte

Brettanomyces yeast is often present, giving these beers an earthy note.

Aging in barrels can take from 18 to 36 months.

Brouwerij Bockor

Barrels, called *foudres*, used for aging are often over 100 years old.

Fl

Brouwerij Rodenbach

Typically, only used wine barrels are employed in the aging of Flanders red ales.

The Lost Abbey (Port Brewing Company)

Panil

It is sometimes referred to as a Flemish red ale.

The Bruery

Acidic

Food Pairing

| Shellfish | Egg dishes | Mussels | Tangy cheese |

Altbier

Origin: Germany
Color: 11–17 SRM
ABV: 4.5–5.2%
IBU: 35–50
Glassware: stange

Perhaps one of the world's oldest styles, Altbier still maintains a chic, hip reputation. Even today, it is a fine choice in any beer hall in Düsseldorf.

TANTALIZING COPPER

In the idyllic brewing climate of Düsseldorf, Germany, Altbier has found a comfortable home. When the rest of Germany turned to lagers, this hybrid style borrowed the best from both worlds: it undergoes warm fermentation, then is cold-conditioned for several weeks. The body is clear, a tantalizing copper with some versions nearing a deeper reddish brown. It is capped with a solid tan head. The nose emits an undercurrent of the characteristic ale fruits, generally overshadowed by a soft malt body. A sip reveals a clean, crisp maltiness in tandem with the snappy bitterness of hops, all driving to a dry finish. Medium-bodied, smooth, and drinkable, it is a great session beer.

Three Beers to Try

UERIGE ALTBIER Known as one of the finest of the style, it has big aromatics and a bitter bite. It melds into rich malts, giving a friendly balance of bold flavors.

FRANKENHEIM ALT Boldly hop forward and highly drinkable. Caramelly malts balance before the hops return to the finish.

ALASKAN AMBER A mix of caramel and fruit at the core, the hops take a bit of a backseat to the rich malts.

Most famous in Düsseldorf, Germany.

Widmer Brothers Brewing

Long Trail Brewing Co.

A Sticke is a stronger version of this style.

Uerige Obergärige Hausbrauerei

Brauerei Im Füchschen

This style gained its current name in the 1800s.

Alt

Alaskan Brewing Co.

Smooth

With its roots in the Rhineland, Germany, over 3,000 years ago, it is said that this style has been continuously brewed longer than any other.

Alt means "old," which may refer to the beer's long conditioning time.

Rounded

Düsseldorfer Privatbrauerei Frankenheim

Crisp

Bitter

Food Pairing

Roasted chicken	Grilled salmon	Pork	Burgers

Roggenbier

Origin: Germany
Color: 14–19 SRM
ABV: 4.5–6%
IBU: 10–20
Glassware: mug

An invention of the brewers of Regensburg, Bavaria, Germany, Roggenbier is essentially a Dunkelweizen (see page 104), but with malted rye replacing a portion of the wheat. That addition makes for a spicy, refreshing choice.

AN EXILE RETURNS

In 1516 Roggenbier fell out of production when rye was exiled from the brewhouse by beer purity laws, which limited the ingredients used in beer production to water, barley, yeast, and hops. However, following a slow comeback in the 1980s, a few well-crafted examples of the Roggenbier style exist today.

In color, this style runs from light orange to a coppery brown. A firm, creamy head caps a typically unfiltered body. Aromas of freshly baked rye bread, soft spices, earth, and yeast predict the palate. Mild fruits mingle with the rye and the bready, yeasty, and spicy center. The finish is tangy, slightly bitter, and dry.

Three Beers to Try

↓ **WOLNZACHER ROGGENBIER** Yeast on the nose of banana and cloves, continues on the palate, with sweet bread and slightly funky earthiness.

↕ **THURN UND TAXIS ROGGEN** Now brewed by the Paulaner brewery, it pours a dark amber with a beautiful off-white head. Pronounced characteristics of Weizen, with fruits and a smooth, malt center.

↓ **ROGUENBIER RYE** Made entirely from the brewer's—Rogue Ales—very own hops, barley, and rye. Notes of rye, smoke, pepper, and spice with light fruit throughout.

Roggenbier

Banana

Tart

Yeasty

Live Oak Brewing Company

Cloves

After a 500-year period of dormancy, Roggenbier was resurrected by the Spezial brewery in eastern Bavaria in the 1980s.

Roggen is German for "rye."

Rogue Brewery

Rye bread

Rg

Typically brewed with 30–60% rye malt.

Beer Here Brewery

Fürstenhaus Thurn und Taxis

Spicy

Bürgerbräu Wolnzach

Roggenbier declined in the Middle Ages, as rulers outlawed the use of certain grains for brewing to save them for making bread.

Paulaner Brauerei

Roggenbier all but disappeared with the introduction of the *Reinheitsgebot* (Bavarian Beer Purity Law) in 1516, which prohibited rye for brewing.

Food Pairing

Barbecued pork	Sausages	Corned beef

Dubbel

Origin: Belgium
Color: 10–20 SRM
ABV: 6–7.8%
IBU: 15–25
Glassware: goblet

A cool evening and a warm meal make the perfect partners to the malty, spicy, fruity Belgian dubbel.

DARK FRUITS AND SPICE

Rich, robust, malty, yeasty, spicy, fruity, and sweet. And that's just the beginning. Dubbel is an intricate and complex blend of flavors and textures, luring in the drinker from the outset. The aromatics can be fruity, with plums, figs, raisins, and even cherry. The yeast profile on both the nose and the palate has notes of pepper, clove, cinnamon, and nutmeg. A mahogany to russet-brown body is capped by a sticky tan lace that laps the glass like a sturdy sea foam. A medium to full-bodied mouthfeel often blends chewiness with chocolate, rum notes, nuts, caramel, tawny port, and a smooth layer of alcohol. Hops play a supporting role, used solely for balance.

Three Beers to Try

CHIMAY PREMIÈRE   A well-known dubbel worldwide, also known as Chimay Red, it has a complex mosaic of fruit, cinnamon, and herbs with a soft, smooth body.

WESTMALLE DUBBEL   An initial tang, followed by chocolate and warming alcohol. It has a meaty mouthfeel like chestnuts and has a dry finish of lingering dark fruits and raisins.

TRAPPISTES ROCHEFORT 6   The bouquet is bready and spicy, with a thin layer of chocolate. Light and smooth mouthfeel underneath a caramel, fruity, slightly spicy palate.

THE ATOMIC STRUCTURE OF
Dubbel

- Caramelly
- Brewery Ommegang
- Only eight Trappist monasteries exist and they are the only breweries allowed to label their beer as "Trappist beer."
- Dark fruity
- Raisiny
- Port-like
- Brouwerij St. Bernardus
- The origins of the style lie in the Middle Ages.
- Dubbel has its roots in Trappist monasteries, most which still brew today.

Du

- Brasserie de Rochefort
- Dark candy sugar is added to the wort during brewing, which heightens complexity and lightens the body.
- Bières de Chimay
- A dark abbey beer was reformulated in 1926 by Westmalle, to give us the beer that is today styled as dubbel.
- Bierbrouwerij De Koningshoeven
- Brouwerij der Trappisten van Westmalle

Food Pairing

| Beef stew | Game meats | Roasted chicken and pork | Olives |

Flanders Brown

Origin: Belgium
Color: 12-18 SRM
ABV: 4.8-5.2%
IBU: 15-25
Glassware: flute, tulip

This style, also known as oud bruin, can be a shock to the unsuspecting, but with a little forewarning and an open mind this Flemish specialty can be a treat.

MYSTERIOUS AND INTENSE

Blended to achieve different results, Flanders brown allows the brewer to become the artist. It pours brown, often with a hint of ruby, and is capped with a tan head. The nose is a mysterious, intense blend: notes of chocolate, raisins, nuts, sherry, malts, dark fruits, barnyard, wet wool, and leather can all stir together into a shockingly pleasant bouquet. The palate is simplified slightly from the aroma, but there is still an intense interplay of flavors, a forward tartness balanced by fruit and malt sweetness. Typically little bitterness is present, and the overall body is medium, with low carbonation. This outlier on the beer scene is definitely worth seeking out.

Three Beers to Try

GOUDENBAND Made by Liefmans, each bottle of this crimson-brown liquid is wrapped in tissue paper. The funky, horsey nose blends with dark fruit and oak. Balanced fruit and tartness.

LIPS OF FAITH—LA FOLIE Brewed once a year by New Belgium, this version of the style ages for one to three years. Sour apple and malt on the palate, tart and quenching.

PETRUS OUD BRUIN From Bavik, this beer has a complex barnyard nose with citrus highlights. It is lightly sour, balanced with fruity, malty sweetness, with a refreshingly tart finish.

Sour

Tart

Vinous

Brouwerij Van Steenberge

Unlike in the aging of a Flanders red, Flanders brown also undergoes a period of aging in stainless steel.

Originally brewed in East Flanders.

Brouwerij Bockor

The dark caramel malts add both a depth of color and a prominent maltiness to this style.

Fb

Brouwerij Bavik

Historically brewed as a "provision beer," one that would age and develop if cellared.

Brouwerij Liefmans

New Belgium Brewing Company

Complex

It is less tart than Flanders red, the result is sometimes blended with fruit.

Deschutes Brewery

Food Pairing

| Flemish stew | Game meats | Pork | Aged cheddar |

Belgian Strong Dark Ale

Origin: Belgium
Color: 7-22 SRM
ABV: 7-11%
IBU: 20-50
Glassware: goblet

Seductive, complex, and varied, into this category of dark, smooth, and intense brews fall some of the world's greatest beers.

DARKLY COMPLEX

This beer is deep in color, aromatic on the nose, tempting on the tongue, and delicious on the palate. One brew from this category could crown the top spot on many a beer lover's list. While the style is truly a menagerie of breweries' artistic endeavors, there are a few factors that run throughout. Colors range from a dark amber to deeply brown with rocky heads of ecru to beige. The bouquet is bountiful: raisins, dates, spices, various fruits, caramel, bread, herbs, and pepper. A malty backbone is prevalent and on this lie other ancillary flavors typically layered with a malty sweetness. The alcohol is wisely hidden, but warming and present nonetheless.

Three Beers to Try

CHIMAY GRANDE RÉSERVE (Also called Chimay Blue Cap.) A preeminent example of this style. Sweet malts blend with dark fruit and spices to finish dry. Ages beautifully.

WESTVLETEREN 12 (YELLOW CAP)
Released in the United States in December 2012, the infamous "Westy" had its debut outside the abbey walls. An incredible example of the style, now becoming a bit more easily available.

ROCHEFORT 10 (BLUE CAP) Deep brown with streaks of lace that crawl down the glass. The nose is bready and earthy with raisins, caramel, and cloves. A sweet blend of maltiness on the palate and a dry finish, all concealing a big 11.3% ABV.

- Sweet
- Brouwerij St. Bernardus
- Brouwerij Van Steenberge
- A catch-all classification for dark, Belgian beers with ABV typically above 8%.
- Most can be cellared for over five years.
- Unibroue
- Warming
- Malty
- Trappist versions of the style are typically drier, while Abbey-style and New World renditions are slightly more sweet.
- Brasserie de Rochefort
- Rich
- Quadrupel, or quad, is a sister style, with arguably minute differences.
- Complex
- Some brewers add sugar to thin the body of the beer.
- Bières de Chimay
- Brouwerij Westvleteren (De Sint-Sixtusabdij van Westvleteren)

Bs

Food Pairing

| Short ribs | Game meats | Mushrooms | Washed-rind cheeses |

Weizenbock

Origin: Germany
Color: 15–20 SRM
ABV: 6–8.5%
IBU: 15–30
Glassware: weizen

With a relatively high alcohol content, this wheat beer fits the bill for a cold winter's eve.

WINTER WARMTH

From a Dunkelweizen to a Weizenbock, we continue to climb up the wheat-beer ladder of increasing alcoholic strength, darkness of color, and complexity of flavor. At the top of this scale, the Weizenbock is an intriguing brew. The fruity notes on the nose meld with the grains and yeast to form an immediate impression of depth. There are often the common notes of banana, cloves, and spice, but with a pronounced caramel and malt character. While still highly drinkable and smooth, the blend of fruitiness, heavy maltiness, and sweetish alcohol make this less a thirst-quenching brew than a comforting and warming winter drink.

Three Beers to Try

SCHNEIDER WEISSE TAP 6 UNSER AVENTINUS The characteristic banana and clove meld beautifully with rich caramel and sweet, warming alcohol.

WEIHENSTEPHANER VITUS Pours golden with a bursting nose of bread-like maltiness and hints of fruit and cloves. The palate reflects the nose, with a long and complex finish.

VICTORY MOONGLOW WEIZENBOCK
The incredibly smooth body swims with apple and banana notes, blending with caramel and spices. Deliciously warming and substantial

THE ATOMIC STRUCTURE OF
Weizenbock

Fruity

Caramelly

Brauerei Michael Plank

Bayerische Staatsbrauerei Weihenstephan

Sweet

In 1907, Schneider Weiss Brauhaus created a strong, dark wheat beer that remains the standard of the style.

30%

It is thought that the original bock of Einbeck, Germany, was in fact a Weizenbock, containing around 30% wheat.

Wz

G. Schneider & Sohn

Victory Brewing Company

Creamy

Schneider Aventinus Eisbock is classified as a Weizenbock, but is frozen in the style of an Eisbock, which steps up the alcohol to a hefty 12%.

Brauerei Aying

Smooth

Weizenbock, also known as a wheat Doppelbock, was the ale response to the wildly popular lager, Doppelbock.

Weyerbacher Brewing Company

Food Pairing

| Roasted meats | Grilled vegetables | Blue cheese | Apple desserts |

Belgian Black Ale

Origin: Belgium
Color: 30–40 SRM
ABV: 4–6.2%
IBU: 20–40
Glassware: tulip, snifter, oversized wine glass

Not to be confused with Belgian strong dark ale (see page 116), this one is a true contradiction—smooth and light in texture, but deeply dark in the glass.

LIGHT AND DARK

Despite apparent references to the style dating back to the mid-1500s, Belgian black (also known as Belgian dark ale) has a hazy history. A couple of fairly standard features help to cohere the style: darkness of body and character eloquently blended with Belgian yeast. The result of this blend is a dark, smooth, rich brew, lightened in texture and taste by the fruity, sprightly, often zesty yeasts of Belgium. Spices appear such as anise, coriander, black pepper, and cardamom. Hints of chocolate, coffee, and toffee from the malt bill may be present as well. Highly drinkable, it is a pleasant surprise.

Three Beers to Try

CHAMBLY NOIRE   By Unibroue. The thin body goes down easily, with hints of coffee, roasted malt, and spices. A slight smokiness throughout, ends in a lingering finish.

1554 ENLIGHTENED BLACK ALE   The light body has notes of bitter chocolate, roastiness, and fruit on the palate, with a sweet and bitter balance, and dry finish. By New Belgium.

TILBURG'S DUTCH BROWN ALE
A richly complex brew by the Netherlands' only Trappist brewery, Koningshoeven. Notes of chocolate and toffee play through a sweet, creamy body.

Many beers of this style are released in the cold winter months.

Brouwerij St. Bernardus

Bierbrouwerij De Koningshoeven

Roasty

Also called Belgian dark ale.

Brouwerij Bavik

This style is the home for Belgian beers that don't fit in the dubbel or strong dark ale styles.

Bba

Creamy

1554

Brewery Ommegang

New Belgium Brewing Company's creation, 1554, is titled as such based on a historical reference to a black Belgian beer brewed in that year.

Unibroue

Some beers in this style may be stouts brewed with a Belgian yeast strain.

New Belgium Brewing Company

Spicy

Food Pairing

| Pork chops | Lamb | Chocolate | Meat sandwiches |

LAGERS OF CONTINENTAL EUROPEAN ORIGIN

LAGERS OF CONTINENTAL EUROPEAN ORIGIN

An oft-misunderstood category of beer, the lager family has a rich heritage, only recently overshadowed by mega-conglomerate brewing and its consistent, but uncreative, standardized products. The average beer drinker may think only of these undistinguished pale forms of lager, but there are a vast range of flavorful, clean, tantalizing beers in this category to be discovered and enjoyed.

When categorizing beer, each style falls into either the lager or the ale camp (save a few hybrid exceptions). While ales dominate in terms of varieties of styles, lagers have the stronghold on quantities consumed worldwide. It is this dominance, however, that has tainted the view of many ale fans, leading some to unfairly judge the whole style by its weakest members.

In general terms, a lager is labeled as such because of its cool fermentation, typically 40–45°F (4–7°C), and its extended period of "lagering." This term, which comes from *lager*, meaning "store room" in German, illustrates one of the integral and defining features in the brewing process, separating it from those in the ale category. This longer period of cool aging and the use of bottom-fermenting lager yeast eliminates some of the characteristic fruity elements found in ales and rounds out harsher flavors, resulting in clean, clear flavors, behind which brewing imperfections cannot hide.

The most consumed styles of the world fall into this category of pale lagers. Despite American dominance in the style today, it was from Germany that the brews originated. In the 1400s, Bavarian brewers discovered that the storage of beer in cool caves resulted in a beer that kept well, even through warmer months. Soon, brewers took to fermenting and aging brews in caves, and by 1553 this practice was made law by the Bavarian Duke Albrecht V, the edict banning warm-weather brewing. This eventually all but eliminated the yeasts fermenting at warmer temperatures in the region and, in turn, lager brewing became the primary focus of the area's brewing activity. The first examples were dark, but with the rising popularity of pale ale elsewhere, German brewers, at home and abroad, followed suit and soon pilsner and helles were all the rage. These beers are beautifully clean and balanced, with solid malts, but spicy, sharp bitterness and a quenching, refreshing quality. Vienna lager—spawned from Bohemian pilsner—was akin to the Märzens and Oktoberfest brews of Germany. It is the bock family in which lagers start to pointedly stray from the lighter lager styles. The Maibock is light in color, but richly malty. Bock takes on a bit more color and malt, but is still smooth and satisfying. Doppelbock—the "liquid bread"—comes in even stronger, but subtly so, and can be an almost black-brown. Eisbock is the strongest of the bock bunch, born from methods of freezing to produce a concentrated, sweet, alcoholic sipper. A drinker's preconceptions may be completely shattered with a sip of the darkest of the lager family, Schwarzbier, which, veiled in blackness, remains a clean, crisp, and drinkable dark beer, with notes of bittersweet and nuts.

Lagers will not be as complex as ales, but are no less enjoyable. In their straightforward simplicity, the aromas are distinct, the appearance enticing and the taste delicious.

German Pilsner

Origin: **Germany**
Color: **2–5 SRM**
ABV: **4.5–5.2%**
IBU: **25–45**
Glassware: **pilsner, flute, mug**

When a bright golden lager was born in Bohemia (page 128), it didn't take long for German brewers to see its appeal. They embraced it and made it their own, and today it is the nation's most widely consumed style.

SHEER GOLD

German pilsner pours a beauty—from a crystal, pale straw to a sparkling gold, always capped with a dense puff of bright white. Its sheer, bright body presents a steady stream of carbonation, rushing to aid the lacing head. On the palate there is a crisp, refreshing, assertive hop bitterness. With little else to distract, the bitterness becomes the focal point, but not without a supporting bready malt character. It is an appetizing blend that finishes satisfyingly dry. While similar to the Bohemian version from which it originated, German pilsner is typically more pale, dry, and carbonated, with a slightly less aromatic nose.

Three Beers to Try

BITBURGER PREMIUM PILS Claiming the spot of Germany's number one draft beer, it is pale golden with a crisp, clean bitterness, yet not so much as to drown the pleasant German malt.

JEVER PILSENER Significant hops on the nose, layered with bready malts. A zippy, refreshing bitterness finishes incredibly dry.

PRIMA PILS Perhaps the best American rendition of the style, this floral hop masterpiece from Victory Brewing blends delightfully well with the malts.

THE ATOMIC STRUCTURE OF

German Pilsner

- Brooklyn Brewery
- Clean
- North Coast Brewing Company
- True versions of the style only use noble hops: Hallertauer, Tettnang, Spalt, and Saaz.
- Also called pilsener or pils.
- Trumer Brewery
- Due to its delicate nature, the raw ingredients used to make this style of beer must be top quality.

Gp

- Bitburger Brauerei
- Delicate
- Pils of northern Germany are typically more hop forward and those from the south less so.
- Victory Brewing Company
- Friesisches Brauhaus zu Jever
- Refreshing
- Bitter
- Sharp
- First brought to the German market in 1872 by what is now the Radeberger Brewery.

Food Pairing

| Shellfish | Spicy sausages | Indian food | Fried fish | Jamaican food |

Bohemian Pilsner

**Origin: Bohemia
(Czech Republic)
Color: 3.5-6 SRM
ABV: 4-5.5%
IBU: 35-45
Glassware: pilsner,
flute, mug**

**A Bavarian brewer and a city with a lot
of bad beer spawned the world's most
influential style.**

A NAKED BEER

In 1842 in the city of Plzen, Bohemia, a Bavarian brewmaster created
the palest malt of the age. It allowed the creation of a shining body of
gold—highly flavorful and delicate. One of the more difficult beers to
brew, it is often referred to as "naked," as any brewing imperfections
are immediately apparent. It has a characteristically creamy white
head that sits atop a bubbling pale, sparkling body. Aromas of
complex, bready malts blend with the spicy, floral hops, typically
of the Saaz variety. German and Bohemian pilsners share many
similarities, but the Bohemian version is slightly darker in color, less
carbonated, and more aromatic than its sister style from Germany.

Three Beers to Try

PILSNER URQUELL *Urquell* means "original source"
in German. This classic, brewed by Plzensky Prazdroj, is full, flavorful,
and bitter with an eloquently balancing sweet malt.

BUDWEISER BUDVAR (Marketed as Czechvar in
the United States.) This beer is full-bodied burnished gold with a bold
bouquet of spicy hops and sweet bread. Less bitter than some pilsners
on the palate, and smooth.

SAMUEL ADAMS NOBLE PILS This offering
from the Boston Beer Company is a bit more hoppy than is typical for
the style, but is a perfectly refreshing, spicy, slightly citric blend.

Pivovary Staropramen

Clean

Great Lakes Brewing Company

Ironically, Bohemian pilsner was invented by two Bavarians, Martin Steltzer and Josef Groll.

Plzensky Prazdroj

Also known as Czech pilsner.

Invented in 1842 in the city of Pilsen (Plzen), in Bohemia (now part of the Czech Republic).

The Boston Beer Company

Lagunitas Brewing Company

Delicate

Bop

A blond lager by Pilsner Urquell to this day uses the yeast strain from the original pilsner.

Budweiser Budvar Brewery

Refreshing

Sharp

Bitter

Initially a word to describe the specific beer from Pilsen, pilsner came to describe a whole category.

Food Pairing

Shellfish	Spicy sausages	Indian food	Salmon	Ham

Helles

Origin: Germany
Color: 3–5 SRM
ABV: 4.7–5.4%
IBU: 16–22
Glassware: pilsner, flute, mug

Some say creativity works best under pressure. When Bavaria feared losing the German beer drinker to Czech pilsner, helles was born.

A MUNICH MUGFUL

Pleasingly golden, a bright, shimmering body of translucent yellow, confidently capped with a rocky froth of white, helles makes for a picture-perfect pint. The sight is beautiful and the palate well balanced—having a quiet supporting note of hops, and a more spotlighted sweet, bready maltiness. The medium body and smooth mouthfeel clearly explain the popularity of this style in the beer halls of Munich. It is more malty and less bitter than its inspiration, pilsner, yet maintains a quaffable quality the whole mug through.

Three Beers to Try

WEIHENSTEPHANER ORIGINAL From the brewery founded in 1040 comes an example that typifies the style. Malt forward, but balanced, smooth, and refreshing.

HOFBRÄU ORIGINAL Brewed by Munich's famous Hofbräuhaus, this beer is golden in color and substantial, with a forward maltiness.

SPATEN PREMIUM LAGER From the creator of the style, this beer has a bready, sweet malt body, balanced with a zip of hops.

THE ATOMIC STRUCTURE OF

Helles

Pronounced *hell-us*

Hacker-Pschorr Bräu

Spaten-Franziskaner-Bräu

Invented by Munich's Spaten-Franziskaner-Bräu on March 21, 1894.

Löwenbräu

Hell means "bright" or "light" in German.

Hell-us

H

Malty

Soft

Paulaner Brauerei

Subtle

Ur, meaning "original," is often added to illustrate the authentic nature of a particular brewery's helles.

Bright

Cleansing

Hofbräu München

Often served in liter-sized glass mugs.

Bayerische Staatsbrauerei Weihenstephan

Food Pairing

| Light seafood | Sausages | Creamy egg dishes |

Dortmunder Export

Origin: Germany
Color: 4-6 SRM
ABV: 4.8-6%
IBU: 23-30
Glassware: pilsner, flute, pint

From Dortmund, the largest city in Germany's industrial region of Ruhr, comes a hearty brew, crafted for the tough workers of the day.

HEARTY AND REFRESHING

A beer with a heritage always seems to taste better. In the industrial town of Dortmund in the 19th century, mining was king, and the miners thirsted for a hearty, yet refreshing brew. Dortmunder export is hoppier than a helles, but less so than a pilsner. The result is a well-balanced quencher. The body is typically a shade of gold with a lasting head, and the innocent aroma is a faint mixture of hops and slightly sweet malt. The balance continues on first sip, which evokes a rich, sometimes caramelly, malt character and a present, but not bold, layer of hops. Typically it racks in at about 5.5 percent ABV, just enough to take the edge off after a hard day at the coal face.

Three Beers to Try

BALTIKA #7 EXPORT Pours bright gold and has a pleasing, bready nose. Slight citrus and lemon grass hops guide a clean finish.

DAB ORIGINAL One of the few beers of this style still produced in Dortmund—light maltiness, clean, and as balanced as it should be.

GREAT LAKES DORTMUNDER GOLD On the dark side for this style at a deep amber, this world champion is complex, well-balanced, and has a dry finish.

Sometimes abbreviated to "export."

Dortmunder Actien-Brauerei

Old Dominion Brewing Company

Today, only two large breweries survive in Dortmund: Dortmunder Actien-Brauerei and Dortmunder Union Brauerei.

The style has faded in recent years.

Two Brothers Brewing Company

Hearty

De

Baltika Breweries

Smooth

In the late 1870s, one of the best beers of the style was made a bit stronger to avoid spoilage and thus dubbed "export."

Balanced

Great Lakes Brewing Company

Malty like a helles, hoppy like a pilsner.

Quenching

Brauerei Aying

Food Pairing

| Steak | Burgers | Thai food |

Maibock

Origin: Germany
Color: 6–11 SRM
ABV: 6.3–7.5%
IBU: 23–35
Glassware: mug

In the world of bocks, Maibock is a newcomer, but the changes that it has undergone since its birth have made it the perfect pint with which to usher in spring.

MALTY AND SATISFYING

With the origins of bock brewing in the 14th century (see traditional bock, page 144), Maibock was a relative latecomer. The malting innovations that came in the 19th century and affected the color of many styles had an influence on this type of beer as well. Modern Maibocks are burnished gold to light amber in color with a clear body and a lacy, creamy, white head. Rich maltiness is the focus, but tempered slightly by a touch more bitterness than others in the bock family. It is well-balanced in body and lacks any roasted or caramel notes. It aims to be satisfying and substantial without being heavy or overly complex.

Three Beers to Try

EINBECKER MAI-UR-BOCK This well-balanced, deeply amber brew is a testament to time-honored tradition.

HOFBRÄU MAIBOCK This classic pours a glittering copper-red, thickly capped with a beige head. Rich, sweet malts harmonize with a hop note on the clean finish.

ST. BOISTEROUS Smooth, full-bodied, and drinkable. This brew from Victory is clean, refreshing, and well-built.

- Hacker-Pschorr Bräu
- Brauerei Aying
- Bready
- *Maibock* means "May bock," this style was originally only made during early or mid spring.
- Also called *heller* or *helles bock*, which means pale (or light) bock.
- Capital Brewery Co.
- Malty
- Stronger than Vienna lagers, Oktoberfest, or Munich helles.
- Victory Brewing Company
- Satisfying
- Elias Pilcher came to Munich from Einbeck, in 1614, and brewed a strong beer called "Maibock."
- Rich
- Hofbräu München
- Light
- Einbecker Brauhaus

Mk

Food pairing

| Spicy Thai food | Roasted pork | Shellfish | Barbecue | Carrot cake |

Märzen/Oktoberfest

Origin: Germany
Color: 7-14 SRM
ABV: 4.8-5.9%
IBU: 20-28
Glassware: pint, mug

Brewed in March (Märzen) and stored until Oktoberfest, this style of beer is the perfect way to celebrate the turn of the seasons.

HISTORIES INTERTWINED

The fathers of this style and Vienna lager were fellow brewmasters, giving the two styles intertwined histories. Based on Anton Dreher's work with Vienna lager, the Sedlmayrs of the Spaten-Franziskaner-Bräu in Munich gave Märzen its fame.

The lines between Märzen and Oktoberfest have become blurred, so it makes sense to group them together. Both Märzen and Oktoberfest beers are rich in character, with prominence placed on the malts and just enough hop bitterness to balance. They are quite smooth with mixtures of fresh-baked bread, toffee, malt sweetness, and a dash of spiciness. The truest versions are clear and deep gold to reddish amber in color with an off-white, rocky head. They are creamy, complex, and satisfying.

Three Beers to Try

SPATEN OKTOBERFEST UR-MÄRZEN
Called *Ur-Märzen* (original Märzen), for a reason; the brewery that created the style brewed this one first. Pouring crystal clear copper, it is a hearty, balanced, satisfying classic.

AYINGER OKTOBER FEST-MÄRZEN
Another exemplary offering of the style. It is pure balance: malty with enough bitterness, rich, but clean and satisfying, and not heavy.

HACKER-PSCHORR ORIGINAL OKTOBERFEST   With a blend of toasty, sweet malts and fresh hops, this one is silky smooth with a clean finish.

THE ATOMIC STRUCTURE OF
Märzen/Oktoberfest

Hofbräu München

Hacker-Pschorr Bräu

Märzen means "March," in German, traditionally this style was brewed in spring and stored until Oktoberfest.

Great Lakes Brewing Company

This style would be stored in caves through the hot summer months.

Malty

Mo

Soft

Paulaner Brauerei

Creamy

Before refrigeration, March was typically the last month of brewing in Germany, as the summer months would be too warm.

Spaten-Franziskaner-Bräu

Brauerei Aying

Rich

Balanced

Satisfying

Märzen was first served at Munich's annual beer festival, Oktoberfest, in 1872.

Food Pairing

| Grilled foods | Pizza | Burgers | Sausages |

Vienna Lager

Origin: Austria
Color: 10–16 SRM
ABV: 4.5–5.9%
IBU: 18–30
Glassware: mug, flute, pilsner, tulip

Influenced by the pale beers of the early 19th century, Vienna lager was, in part, Austria's answer to Bohemian pilsner.

HOPPY AND DRY

With origins in Vienna, Austria, this style of lager has spread through the world and is now brewed elsewhere much more than in its birthplace. It is bright amber to copper in color, with a sticky off-white to tan head, and clean aromas of sweet malt and toastiness that emerge on the nose. While it and its German sister, the Märzen/Oktoberfest style (page 136), have a host of similarities, there are a few distinguishing factors. It is slightly lower in gravity, a bit more heavily hoppy, and a little drier. Vienna lager leans less toward malt than a Märzen or Oktoberfest and is, in turn, slightly less rich.

Three Beers to Try

SAMUEL ADAMS BOSTON LAGER From the Boston Beer Company comes its flagship. First brewed in 1984, it has helped popularize craft beer in the United States ever since.

ELIOT NESS This stronger-than-usual version of the style, pours bright copper and has a well-built malt character that balances to become quenching. Produced by Great Lakes.

NEGRA MODELO Deep amber, bordering on copper, its palate is smooth, sweetly malty, and bready. Only slightly bitter, it finishes all malt.

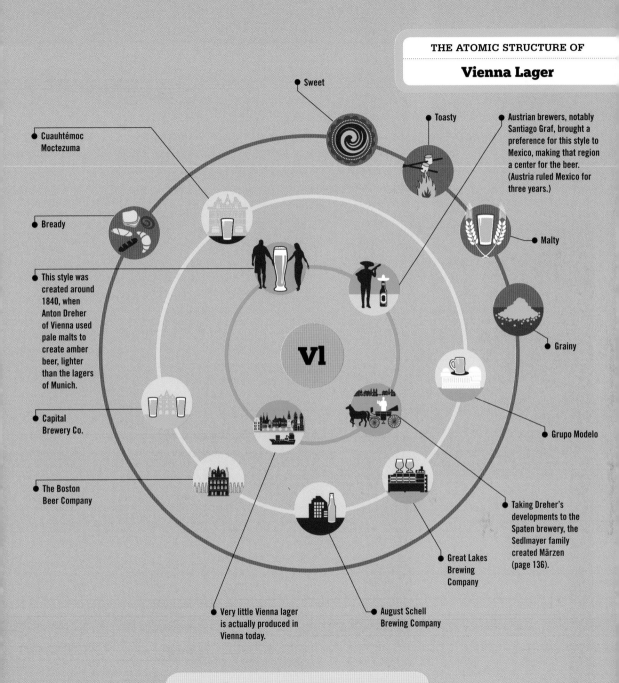

Sweet

Toasty

Austrian brewers, notably Santiago Graf, brought a preference for this style to Mexico, making that region a center for the beer. (Austria ruled Mexico for three years.)

Cuauhtémoc Moctezuma

Bready

Malty

This style was created around 1840, when Anton Dreher of Vienna used pale malts to create amber beer, lighter than the lagers of Munich.

Grainy

Vl

Capital Brewery Co.

Grupo Modelo

The Boston Beer Company

Taking Dreher's developments to the Spaten brewery, the Sedlmayer family created Märzen (page 136).

Great Lakes Brewing Company

Very little Vienna lager is actually produced in Vienna today.

August Schell Brewing Company

Food Pairing

| Grilled meats | Grilled vegetables | Ham | Fried fish |

Kellerbier

Origin: Germany
Color: 10–20 SRM
ABV: 5–5.5%
IBU: 25–35
Glassware: mug, stange

A rarity in today's beer world, Kellerbier's characteristic haze makes it distinctly different from a family of crystal clear lagers.

A CLOUDY BREW

A historical style, with its origins in Franconia, Germany, traditionally Kellerbier is brewed and then matured long, cool, and slow in oak casks with the bung or stopper not completely closed. This allows the carbon dioxide that is created to escape as it is produced, leading to a cloudy, hazy brew, with very light carbonation. It has a deep amber body and most often the head is non-existent—when it is present it is a bright white layer of airy fluff. A delicate nose of aromatic, noble hops transitions to more intense hop bitterness on the palate. This beer is not pasteurized, which results in a short shelf life and means that there are only a few examples of Kellerbier generally available far from the breweries that make it.

Three Beers to Try

ST. GEORGEN BRÄU KELLER BIER Pours amber-brown with a nice head of beige. Complexly malty, the hops provide roundness and balance, and an earthy, hop bitterness.

PILZILLA Brewed by Voodoo, this beer has a cloudy, golden body, topped with a perfectly retaining white head. The bouquet is herbal and earthy, with a floral note upon first sip. Long, bitter finish.

SAMUEL ADAMS ALPINE SPRING While perhaps not solely categorized as a Kellerbier, it does show several characteristics, namely being unfiltered. It maintains a soft malt character and a bitter hop bite. By the Boston Beer Company.

THE ATOMIC STRUCTURE OF

Kellerbier

Kb

- Brauerei Hofstetten
- Mahr's Bräu
- Still brewed and enjoyed in its region of origin, Franconia, Germany.
- Zwickelbier and Zoiglbier are very similar styles.
- Kulmbacher Brauerei
- *Kellerbier* literally means "cellar beer."
- Flat
- Smooth
- The Boston Beer Company
- St. Georgen Bräu
- Sometimes this style is filtered and carbonation added in order to ship to markets outside of the immediate area in which it is brewed.
- Hazy
- Before refrigeration it was matured in deep, cool caves.
- Voodoo Brewing Co.
- Bitter

Food Pairing

German food	Sausages	Burgers	Spicy food

Rauchbier

Origin: Germany
Color: 12-22 SRM
ABV: 4.8-6%
IBU: 20-30
Glassware: stange

Rauchbier is just one style of smoked beer, a category that encompasses a wide range of beers (including ales) brought together by a delicious undercurrent of smoke.

RETAINING THE SMOKE

In early brewing, all beer styles had a touch of smoke as a result of the kilning process. Following the introduction of techniques to eliminate the smoke, some brewers retained the smokiness, even increasing the degree to which smoke was present. Many smoke-influenced styles of today draw on this tradition. While Rauchbiers are lagers, many of today's smoked beers are ales.

The Rauchbier base is typically a darkened Märzen, bright copper to dark brown in color. On the palate, a smoke layer gently filters through the sweet, toasted maltiness. It is medium-bodied and smooth, with the characteristically clean lager feel.

Three Beers to Try

AECHT SCHLENKERLA RAUCHBIER MÄRZEN The aroma is immediately bonfire smokiness, followed by chewy malts and bold hops. The smoke layer lingers throughout, becoming more inviting with each sip.

EISENBAHN RAUCHBIER Aromas of caramel, toffee, and smoke are echoed by a similar flavor profile. A sweet, malty finish lingers, slightly more prominently than the smoke.

SPEZIAL RAUCHBIER Mellow smoke and toasty malt notes interplay through a smooth, medium-bodied brew. Long, dry, slightly smoky finish.

THE ATOMIC STRUCTURE OF

Rauchbier

Rauch means "smoke" in German.

Eisenbahn

Brauerei Spezial

Toasty

Some breweries produce the smoked malt that they use in their Rauchbier.

Smoky

Jack's Abby Brewing

Malty

Rauchbiers originate from the city of Bamburg in the Franconia region of Germany.

Bacon

Smk

While the initial smoke flavor can be surprising and strong, once the palate adjusts, this can be quite a drinkable brew.

The Boston Beer Company

Brauerei Heller-Trum/Schlenkerla

Victory Brewing Company

The wood used in the kilning process is typically beech.

Food Pairing

| Barbecue | Bacon | Ham | Smoked salmon | Sausages |

Traditional Bock

Origin: Germany
Color: 14-22 SRM
ABV: 6.2-7.2%
IBU: 20-27
Glassware: pokal, mug, stange

A rich, satisfying brew, this style became a Munich mainstay with a little help from a brewer from Einbeck.

HOP-RESTRAINED MALTINESS

Some people have the best of luck. Einbeck in central Germany has soft water, great hops, a historical cultivation of wheat and barley, quality malting techniques, and brewers disciplined to know only to brew in winter. These are the ingredients that make for an incredible beer, one from which several sub-styles have stemmed over the years. Bock is almost entirely malt-focused, the hops reining it in just enough to avoid oversweetness. It is clear and typically copper to deep brown with a lacy, fluffy head. Long lagering produces a smooth, rich, and creamy mouthfeel and the alcohol content makes for a strong, satisfying beer. It has a toasty, bready character with faint notes of caramel.

Three Beers to Try

EINBECKER UR-BOCK DUNKEL Pours an amber-edged copper with a tan head. On the palate are sweet malts, notes of caramel, and toastiness. A firm bitterness balances and aids a lingering, dry finish.

AASS BOCK With a brown body and a bursting bouquet of bready malts, this brew transitions through a smooth mouthfeel of caramel and malts to a sweet finish.

SAMUEL ADAMS WINTER LAGER A blend of spices are added to this wheat bock, to create a slightly different take on the traditional style—a rich blend of malt, hops, and spices.

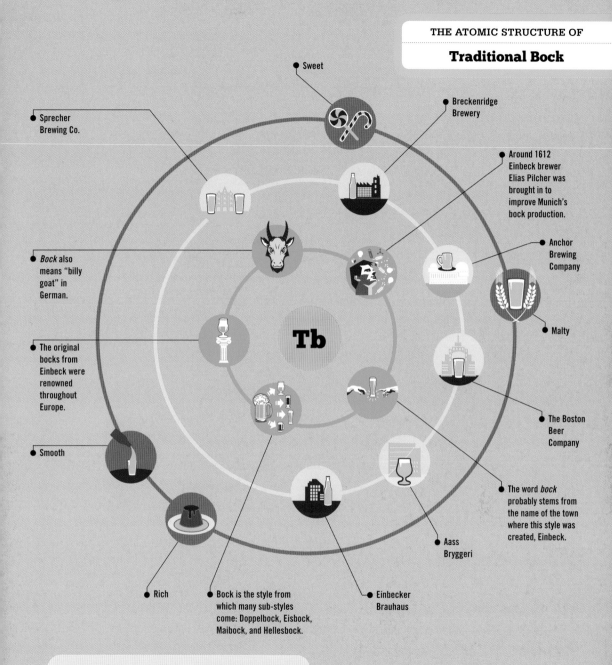

Sweet

Breckenridge Brewery

Sprecher Brewing Co.

Around 1612 Einbeck brewer Elias Pilcher was brought in to improve Munich's bock production.

Anchor Brewing Company

Bock also means "billy goat" in German.

Tb

Malty

The original bocks from Einbeck were renowned throughout Europe.

Smooth

The Boston Beer Company

The word *bock* probably stems from the name of the town where this style was created, Einbeck.

Aass Bryggeri

Rich

Bock is the style from which many sub-styles come: Doppelbock, Eisbock, Maibock, and Hellesbock.

Einbecker Brauhaus

Food Pairing

Barbecue	Fried chicken	Game meats	Duck	Custard

Munich Dunkel

Origin: Germany
Color: 14-28 SRM
ABV: 4.5-5.6%
IBU: 16-30
Glassware: pilsner, mug

Dunkels originated in Bavaria over 500 years ago. Complex, but not heavy or strong, beers of this style are delicious—after all, practice makes perfect.

MALTY COLOR AND FLAVOR

A beer from this long-brewed style is typically a deep reddish-brown blend, but sometimes deepening to a dark brown and crowned with a tan, sticky head. The color is rich and stems from the use of Munich malt, which is often the sole malt used in a beer of this style. The aroma is mainly malt, with just a hint of hops. The palate can be beautifully complex, filled with blends of caramel and toffee notes or hints of coffee and chocolate. There is a sweetness in the malt that is delicately balanced by the bitterness of the hops.

Three Beers to Try

AYINGER ALTBAIRISCH DUNKEL
A classic *Altbairisch,* meaning "old Bavarian," is a ruby-edged mahogany. It is an intriguing contrast of sweet, flavorful malts and a refreshing mouthfeel.

SPATEN DUNKEL Highly drinkable, this amber brew makes no bold decisions. It is balanced, malty, but not too sweet, and just enough bite of hops to make for a clean finish.

PENN DARK Softly wafting notes of caramel and fresh bread on the nose continue on the sweet, malty palate. This brew from the Pennsylvania Brewing Company is smooth and satisfying.

This style of beer made Munich famous for brewing.

Caramelly

Harpoon Brewery

Bready

Toffee

In German *dunkel* means "dark."

Chocolaty

Nutty

Munich malt is the primary malt used.

Md

Pennsylvania Brewing Co.

Capital Brewery Co.

Brewing of dunkel can be traced back to the 1500s.

Spaten-Franziskaner-Bräu

Brauerei Aying

Originated in the Bavarian region of Germany.

Hofbräu München

Food Pairing

| Pork | Sausages | Roasted chicken | Mushrooms | Chinese food |

Doppelbock

Origin: Germany
Color: 15–30 SRM
ABV: 6.5–10%
IBU: 12–30
Glassware: pilsner, flute

While not literally double the traditional bock, this strong, hefty version often sustained monks through Lent, earning it the title "liquid bread."

LENTEN FARE

Typically, Lent—the time in early spring between Ash Wednesday and Easter—is a time devoted to ridding vices from one's life. However, the Paulaner monks of the mid 1700s adopted a different type of fast. Forgoing any sustenance besides Doppelbock, they consumed pint after pint of this rich, malty, satisfying brew. Ranging from a deep mahogany to an almost black, and often containing flashes of garnet, this malt-centered style is a meal in a glass. The strength hides slyly in a body of smooth, bread-like malts. The aroma is of a bakery morning, fresh loaves of grainy, rich bread wafts from the glass. After one glass, you too may decide a fast isn't such a bad idea.

Three Beers to Try

SALVATOR The original of the style from Paulaner and still a classic. A light brown crown rests atop glowing amber, rich, sweet malts meld into a balancing bitter.

CELEBRATOR A sticky, light brown head caps a body of very deep brown. Roasty, sweet malt flavors dominate, melding to a bitter, balancing finish. From Aying.

OPTIMATOR Spaten's contribution to the style. A light caramel weaves through the dark brown body in both bouquet and taste. Full and rich, a great representation.

Paulaner's Salvator is lagered in the deepest lager cellar in the world, 72 ft (23 m) below ground.

Spaten-Franziskaner-Bräu

Toasty

Bayerische Staatsbrauerei Weihenstephan

Following the original, Paulaner's Salvator, many Doppelbock brewers chose to end the beer's name in "tor."

Kulmbacher Brauerei

tor

Warming

Malty

Doppelbock was first sold to the public in 1780 by the Paulaner monks.

Db

Tröegs Brewing Company

Rich

The name of this style literally means "double bock." While not actually double the strength of bock, Doppelbock is higher in alcohol than traditional bock.

Brauerei Aying

Satisfying

Like traditional bock (page 144), Doppelbock has its origins in Einbeck, Germany.

Paulaner Brauerei

Food Pairing

Ham	Roasted pork	Game meats	Duck	Chocolate cake

Eisbock

Origin: Germany
Color: 18–30 SRM
ABV: 9–14%
IBU: 25–35
Glassware: snifter, flute, oversized wine glass, weizen

Eisbock entered the world by happy accident, but has since been crafted with extreme care, producing a deliciously complex brew.

ICY CONCENTRATION

While every story in beer lore has some debate around it, when it comes to the tale of Eisbock's origins, most sources agree on some form of the following account. A brewer or tavern keeper from the German town of Kulmbach left a barrel of bock—probably Doppelbock—outside overnight and when he came to serve it, he found it was partially frozen. He served it anyway and the result was strong and desirable beer. The removal of the ice had concentrated the flavor and increased the alcohol content, creating an intense and flavorful lager. As with all bocks, malt is at its core, but with the high alcohol content there is also a residual warmth, mixed often with notes of sweetness, spices, or fruit.

Three Beers to Try

KULMBACHER REICHELBRÄU EISBOCK

Seductively dark with a rich, thick head. A nose of blended caramel and dark fruits are indicative of the palate, too. Rich with a warming alcohol throughout.

CAPITAL EISPHYRE
A complex blend of fruit, nuts and spices make up the bouquet. Rich and smooth, the body is layered with fruits and chocolate, easing into a long, balanced finish.

KUHNHENN RASPBERRY EISBOCK

A beautifully complex sipping beer, with a fine balance between tart and sweet. The raspberry notes overlay a rich, smooth maltiness.

Sweet

Southampton Publick House

Created initially by accident.

Not to be confused with the "ice beer" for which many Canadian breweries are famous.

Alcohol warmth

Malty

Eib

The strength of an Eisbock lends itself to being sipped like a fine liqueur.

Kuhnhenn Brewing Co.

Rich

Schneider Aventinus Weizen-Eisbock is a Weizenbock brewed in the Eisbock manner. As its base beer is a Weizenbock, it is classed as such, but it is also often categorized as an Eisbock.

Complex

It is described as an "ice strong beer."

Capital Brewery Co.

Kulmbacher Brauerei

Food Pairing

Game meats	Roasted pork	Rich desserts	Crème brûlée

Schwarzbier

Origin: Germany
Color: 25–30 SRM
ABV: 3–3.9%
IBU: 22–30
Glassware: flute, pilsner, pint

This beer has been brewed continuously for longer than any other beer in the world, and yet is still surprisingly underappreciated.

BLACK LAGER

Meet Schwarzbier, the lager family's version of a stout. The roasty quality of this beer adds richness and heartiness to a clean, drinkable brew, and separates it from the rest of the lager pack. Similar to Irish dry stout (page 58), it lacks the harshness characteristic of that style. It is typically very dark, and while nearing black often has ruby edges that denote something just on the brink of pure darkness. It has a delicate and contradictory balance between bitter and sweet, heavy and crisp, and dark color and light feel. Often there are notes of nuttiness, toffee, and sweetness, balanced by enough hop bitterness to avoid a sticky, syrupy body. Very drinkable, it is complex while maintaining a highly sessionable quality.

Three Beers to Try

SPRECHER BLACK BAVARIAN LAGER
Almost black with a brown head, this rich brew has notes of dark, bitter chocolate.

KÖSTRITZER SCHWARZBIER A dry, dusty, earthy malt core is surrounded by a soft, smooth mouthfeel and slightly tangy finish.

MÖNCHSHOFF SCHWARZBIER Bold in flavor, this one, dubbed "the original black," melds coffee, chocolate, and roasty malts with a brisk snap of hops. By Kulmbacher.

The Boston Beer Company

The Duck-Rabbit Craft Brewery

Toffee

Probably the longest continually brewed style of beer worldwide.

Bittersweet

Sometimes called "black pilsner."

Nutty

Swb

Records show that Schwarzbier was brewed as early as the 9th century BCE.

Kulmbacher Brauerei

Kulmbach region of Germany produces some of the best examples of the style.

Köstritzer Schwarzbierbrauerei

Sprecher Brewing Co.

Einbecker Brauhaus

Drinkable

Crisp

Schwarz means "black" in German.

Food Pairing

| Barbecue | Roasted meats | Steak | Blackened chicken | Bread pudding |

BEERS OF AMERICAN ORIGIN

BEERS OF AMERICAN ORIGIN

American beer has a sordid, but influential past. Today's most consumed style of beer worldwide is essentially an American brainchild. Yellow, light, fizzy, and nearing flavorless, this American adjunct has grown to dominate beer culture globally. And yet, running parallel to the mega brewing conglomerates of the land, smaller scale producers have always been a persistent, passionate bunch—today a healthy, vibrant group with a growing influence on the world of craft beer.

If faced with the American version of a beer style, a likely bet is that the result is an amped-up, stronger, hoppier version of the original style. In some categories, an extreme artistic bent has spawned entirely new and intriguing styles, and has helped make the American beer landscape one of the most interesting in the world. The first resurgence of interest in craft beer came in the late 1970s, sparked by the legalization of home brewing. Slow growth through the 80s and 90s has now gained incredible momentum and while large, domestic light lagers still dominate, drinkers are demanding more quality and more choice every day.

Ale styles with origins in America are often confusingly named the same as their British cousins, but frequently the similarities end there. Brown ales of the American tradition are bolder and hoppier. American pale ale is snappy and bursting with citrus, grapefruit, and pine. The IPA is nearly unrecognizable, with copious amounts of American hops, bursting with up-front bitterness. This style is arguably the greatest source of American influence in the brewing world. America's obsession with hops has spread through the craft beer world, where the palates have continually culled the most bitter of brews, birthing the much-loved imperial or double IPA. Following in Belgian footsteps, American brewers have boldly experimented with wild yeast strains, developing some of the funkiest, most complex, most interesting beers in the industry. The American stout category becomes a catch-all for black, viscous, rich brews, but often the distinctions within the style can be wide, individual varieties focusing on coffee, chocolate, and even fruit. Barrel aging these beers has become an American signature, defined separately and more specifically on pages 208–209.

Beyond the world-dominating American lager style, the nation has birthed two additions to the lager family: the long-lost pre-Prohibition lager, whose steady rise in American craft pubs across the nation has garnered it a bit of attention, and the best-forgotten American malt liquor, a high gravity, boozy bomb of a beer.

Most beers are classed as either an ale or a lager, and yet a couple of pure American inventions use the best of both worlds resulting in unique hybrids. Cream ale, born from climactic conditions that disallowed typical lager brewing, is brewed with top-fermenting ale yeast then cold-conditioned, resulting in a clean, refreshing quencher. California common, known broadly as steam beer, is another such American brainchild. This uses bottom-fermenting lager yeast, specifically California lager yeast that works best at warmer, ale-like temperatures.

American Lager

Origin: United States
Color: 2–3 SRM
ABV: 2.8–4.2%
IBU: 5–14
Glassware: pint

Snubbed by many in the craft beer community, this, the world's most consumed style, has its place in the world of beer.

CLEAN AND BRIGHT

As would be supposed, this style—the style that many worldwide automatically call to mind when they think of beer—is light. In body, aroma, flavor, color, calories, and alcohol. The craft beer world scowls at its inherent non-flavor. And yet, there is an occasion for everything.

This light and refreshing beer is pale straw yellow with a bright white, frothy head that quickly disappears. It goes down easily, with carbonation enough to cleanse and few dominant flavors. There are perhaps just hints of a floral hop. To the beer drinker who wants a sessionable beer, this pairs better than most with a ball game or a hot summer's day: Cheers!

Three Beers to Try

MILLER LITE Introduced in 1975, this is one of the original low-calorie beers.

BUDWEISER First brewed in 1876, Budweiser is now brewed by Anheuser-Busch, the world's largest brewer. Dubbed the "king of beers," it is a best-selling beer.

RED STRIPE JAMAICAN LAGER Its brand owned by Diageo (Guinness's owner), this version of the style receives broader acceptance by the beer-drinking community than some others

THE ATOMIC STRUCTURE OF

American Lager

Simple

Grupo Modelo

Pabst Brewing Company

American light lager, a subset of this style, must have at least 25% fewer calories than "standard" lager.

World's best selling lager.

Brewed with up to 40% adjuncts (added ingredients).

Coors Brewing Company

Aml

Drinkable

Desnoes & Geddes

Refreshing

The increase in adjuncts came from a desire to bring brewing costs down.

Brewing with corn and rice adjuncts dates back to 1540 in the United States.

Light

Thin

Miller Brewing Co.

Anheuser-Busch

Food Pairing

| Salad | Barbecue | Pizza | Burgers |

Pale Lager

Origin: United States
Color: 2–8 SRM
ABV: 4.3–5%
IBU: 13–23
Glassware: pilsner, pint

A stepped-up version of typical American lagers, this style has a bit more build, but remains ultimately easy-drinking and refreshing in character.

MORE MALT, MORE STRENGTH

With an ambiguous name and just a few simple differentiating factors, pale lager is a close kin to American lager. However, with a higher malt bill, sometimes no adjuncts at all, and a higher alcoholic strength, this style has garnered a following with a claim to more refined tastes. With globalization and consolidation, European versions have become as popular in the United States as domestic ones. In appearance, this style has much the same straw-yellow color as American lager and a white, diminishing head. It is refreshing, carbonated, and slightly more alcoholic than its cousin, while maintaining a complex hop profile and a bit of malt sweetness.

Three Beers to Try

LONGBOARD ISLAND LAGER Produced by Kona since 1998, this malty refresher has notes of spicy hops.

ICHIBAN Billed as "all-malt," this beer—meaning "number one"—has a crisp body and a clean finish. Made by the Japanese brewer, Kirin.

STELLA ARTOIS Brewed in Leuven, Belgium. Clear, pale straw in color with a billowing bright white head.

THE ATOMIC STRUCTURE OF

Pale Lager

Heineken

Clean

Birra Peroni

A catch-all category for lagers that are slightly more complex than American lager.

Examples of this style are brewed across the globe.

Stella Artois

Pl

This style is made by both craft breweries and worldwide conglomerates.

Grolsch

Balanced

The style has grown in popularity as it has evolved from "yellow fizzy beer" to craft beer.

Kirin Brewery Company

Not typically brewed with adjuncts, these beers are sometimes referred to as "all-malt."

Refreshing

Kona Brewing Co.

Crisp

Food Pairing

| Salads | Light fish dishes | Burgers |

American Malt Liquor

Origin: United States
Color: 2-5 SRM
ABV: 6.25-9%
IBU: 12-23
Glassware: pint, mug

With a primary purpose of getting more alcohol per ounce, this style is generally cheap, boozy, and dry.

ADDED SUGAR, HIGHER ALCOHOL

Along similar lines to American lager, this style amps up the alcohol, giving a light-looking brew a substantially boozy kick. With the addition of significant amounts of adjuncts—often simply straight sugar—the simple beer gains in alcoholic strength up to 9 percent. Typically quite cheaply produced, in the United States it is often served in 40-ounce bottles (just over two pints). It is light, pale yellow to light golden in color. A whiff of grains and alcohol on the nose and palate are typical. There is sometimes a hint of bitterness and some residual sweetness. The low quality, high gravity nature of this style does not lend itself to be paired with food. Its primary mission is the most booze for the buck.

Three Beers to Try

STEEL RESERVE Also called "211," this example attempted to distance itself from the malt liquor style by describing itself as a "high gravity lager."

COLT 45 MALT LIQUOR Brewed by Pabst, one of the first of the style to move away from high-end marketing to promoting the alcoholic kick.

OLDE ENGLISH 800 Clear yellow with a lacking head. Smells of grain and slightly of alcohol. Bitter, metallic, and boozy. This beer is made by Miller.

Simple

Clear

Clix is credited with being the first brand of the style, established in the mid 1930s.

Alcohol taste

The style is often sold in 40-oz bottles in the United States and the beer dubbed a "40."

Jos. Schlitz Brewing Co.

Early marketing attempts presented the style as a bit highbrow.

Thin

Am

Saint Ides Brewing Company

Sparkling Stite by Gluek Brewing was one of the first examples of the style, brewed in 1942.

Anheuser-Busch

Miller Brewing Co.

Some U.S. states regulate that beer over a specified percentage of alcohol be dubbed "malt liquor," whether or not the beer is of this style.

Pabst Brewing Company

Steel Brewing Company

Not usually consumed with food.

Pre-Prohibition Lager

Origin: United States
Color: 3–5 SRM
ABV: 3.5–6%
IBU: 25–40
Glassware: pilsner, pint

The criticisms aimed at much American lager today have been unduly applied to this style, which is now enjoying a resurgence in craft breweries across the United States.

A REDISCOVERED STYLE

January 16, 1920 would forever change the landscape of American beer. With the advent of Prohibition and then its end, 13 years later, lager in the United States became weaker, thinner, and brewed with much higher proportions of adjuncts. However, as the craft beer scene has begun to thrive again, the brews of old have started to stage a comeback.

With higher hop rates, this pale yellow to light amber beer comes with a bitter punch much greater than the standard American lager of today. While adjuncts are still used, typically of rice or corn, it is still more full-bodied and malty. A well-built, refreshing alternative to thinner, weaker brews.

Three Beers to Try

FULL SAIL SESSION LAGER Served in a "stubby" 11-oz (half pint) bottle, this smooth throwback has both flavor and refreshment. Lemon notes clean the palate to a light, zesty finish.

SCHELL'S DEER BRAND Formerly "Original," the brewery's flagship has been brewed since before Prohibition. Crisp, clean, and simple.

COORS BATCH 19 A 21st-century version of the lager brewed before Prohibition times. This new take on the style is deep gold and balanced with a nice hop snap.

THE ATOMIC STRUCTURE OF

Pre-Prohibition Lager

Lucky Bucket
Brewing Company

Higher hop rates
were typical in
lagers before
Prohibition.

Matt Brewing
Company

Flavorful

Also called classic
American pilsner.

Genesee
Brewing
Company

Grainy

The use of
flaked maize
was common
in the original
beers of this
style.

Ppl

Coors
Brewing
Company

Some examples
have been brewed
since before
Prohibition, others
mimic those early
recipes.

German
immigrants,
making best use
of the available
raw materials,
were instrumental
in developing this
style.

Full Sail
Brewing Co.

August Schell
Brewing
Company

Balanced

Bitter

Crisp

Food Pairing

| Sausages | Burgers | Salads | Cajun dishes |

American Blonde/Golden Ale

Origin: United States
Color: 3-6 SRM
ABV: 3.8-6%
IBU: 15-28
Glassware: pint, mug

Here's another candidate to choose for converting a stubborn palate from fizzy, yellow beer to something more substantial and satisfying.

SUMMERTIME QUENCHER

From first glance to last sip, this style seems built for refreshment—a sublime drink for a summer's day. A bright golden clarity invites the drinker to quench. Upon first gulp it is smooth, well-carbonated, and refreshing. There is an underlying malt sweetness layered with a tempered hop flavor, often of lemongrass and florals, and very little bitterness. Approachable, versatile, and well-built, this style is simple and direct in its object: to quench and refresh. This style is comparable to Kölsch (page 78).

Three Beers to Try

SUMMER LOVE ALE This beer from Victory is an ideal summer quencher. Slightly hoppy, with floral and lemon notes.

SOMERSAULT ALE Slightly cloudy, its golden body and fluffy head are a picture of a summer sky. Nicely citric with floral and grassy hop notes. By New Belgium.

TWILIGHT SUMMER ALE A perfect balance of flavor and refreshment. The hops of this ale from Deschutes are of grass and lemon, and the finish is clean.

THE ATOMIC STRUCTURE OF
American Blonde/Golden Ale

Ska Brewing
Company

Kona Brewing Co.

Designed as a
"transition" beer
for those new to the
world of craft beer.

This style
has some
similarities
to a Kölsch.

Victory
Brewing
Company

This style may
use an array of
hops, while its
sister style, the
German Kölsch,
typically uses
German hop
varieties.

Ab

Deschutes
Brewery

Sessionable

The word "summer"
is often used in the
naming of beers of
this style, marketing
their refreshing,
quenching quality.

New Belgium
Brewing
Company

Bright

Refreshing

Lemon

It is common for beers of this
style to be released in late
spring or early summer.

Food Pairing

Salads	Light foods	Fish

Cream Ale

Origin: United States
Color: 3–10 SRM
ABV: 4.5–5.5%
IBU: 15–25
Glassware: pint

Essentially an American lager brewed as an ale, this version was born when typical lagering wasn't an option.

REVIVAL OF PRE-PROHIBITION STYLE

Prohibition wreaked havoc on beer production in the United States and cream ale was one of the victims. What had been a lively, carbonated, and refreshingly crisp ale alternative to American lagers in pre-Prohibition years, became just another fizzy, yellow, and forgettable brew. However, with microbreweries' interest in the style, there has been a new generation of well-crafted examples.

Cream ales are light, ranging from pale, clear yellow to a gentle medium gold. The nose is mild with just hints of hops and fruit. The taste is crisp and clean, characteristically refreshing with slight bitterness. While not overly complex or especially interesting, it can be a perfect partner to a day spent in the sun.

Three Beers to Try

SPOTTED COW One of the style's finest examples, it is a surprisingly complex brew, with initial wafts of fruit and hops finishing through a malt core to a refreshing end. Made by New Glarus.

SUMMER SOLSTICE Self-styled as the "cream soda for adults," this beer by Anderson Valley is incredibly drinkable, smooth, and refreshingly simple.

SWEET ACTION From the Sixpoint Brewery, Brooklyn, New York, comes a hybrid of a hybrid. While it doesn't fit squarely in any category, it is closest here, where the spicy, fruity complexity is trumped only by its perfect drinkability.

THE ATOMIC STRUCTURE OF
Cream Ale

- Genesee Brewing Company
- Clean
- Mild
- Great "lawn-mowing beer."
- Originally known as "American sparkling ale."
- Sessionable
- New Glarus Brewing Co.
- Refreshing
- Crisp
- Anderson Valley Brewing Company
- Some brewers mix lager and ale yeast strains.
- Sixpoint Brewery
- Terrapin Beer Co.
- Big brewer's versions tend to be thin, lacking flavor, and less hoppy than those of craft brewers.
- Narragansett Brewing Company
- Sometimes adjunct grains are used in order to make this beer lighter.

Cr

Food Pairing

| Salads | Light fish dishes | Aged Asiago cheese |

Gluten-free

Origin: As base style
Color: As base style
ABV: As base style
IBU: As base style
Glassware: As base style

With the increasing demand for gluten-free foods, it was simply a matter of time before brewers created a range of beers to suit the dietary needs of many beer drinkers.

TASTE WITHOUT GLUTEN

Much to the relief of the gluten-intolerant beer drinker, beers brewed without gluten are not only growing in popularity, but are becoming available in an increasing range of base styles. Many beer drinkers with gluten intolerance are able to consume only beer in which the gluten content is less than 20 parts per million. Unfortunately, in early versions many of the beers that were made low in gluten were also not very flavorful. Recently, however, a few breweries have begun to focus on producing offerings that are both acceptable for gluten-intolerant drinkers and downright tasty.

Three Beers to Try

PRAIRIE PATH GOLDEN ALE By Two Brothers, this refreshing barley-based golden ale is bready with floral, grassy hops. Very drinkable.

SHAKPARO ALE Brewed from sorghum and millet and marketed as African-style, this beer by Sprecher is sweet and fruity. Perfect for the warmer months: refreshing, light, and sessionable.

OMISSION PALE ALE A fine choice for a pale ale, whether you're gluten-free or not. It pours orange, and the palate is initially hoppy, with citrus and caramel malts trailing behind.

THE ATOMIC STRUCTURE OF

Gluten-free

Widmer Brothers Brewing

Dogfish Head Brewery

Lakefront Brewery produced the first U.S. Government-certified gluten-free beer.

The taste of gluten-free beers varies according to the style of the product.

Omission Beer

Gf

New Planet Beer

Two Brothers Brewing Company

Gluten-free beers use adjunct grains such as sorghum, rice, and buckwheat.

Sprecher Brewing Co.

The description "gluten-free" is often used for beer with very low levels of gluten, but which are not necessarily completely lacking in gluten.

 This entry doesn't include food pairings or tasting notes, as these depend on the beer's base style. Try looking up the style of your gluten-free beer for food pairing suggestions.

American Style Wheat

Origin: United States
Color: 3-6 SRM
ABV: 4-5.5%
IBU: 15-30
Glassware: weizen, pint

For a nation that continues its transition to drinking better beer, this take on the German Weissbier style makes a great bridge to the world of craft beers.

A RUSHING STREAM

Light, refreshing, crisp, and drinkable. That's what many Americans have always wanted from their pint of beer, and, with this style, that's exactly what you get. And more. The pour is a pale straw to a bright golden, the head a voluminous tuft of white. At its center, a rushing stream of carbonation. The nose is bright, lightly hoppy with hints of fruit, but lacks the clove or banana esters of its German cousin. It is crisp and refreshing with a smooth, creamy feel. Hops are more noticeable than in a Weissbier (page 86), but they are not heavy or overbearing. This beer has won over many a convert.

Three Beers to Try

ANCHOR SUMMER BEER   Filtered, clean, and crisp, this refresher is the yardstick for the style.

312 URBAN WHEAT   An inviting golden with a thick foam. Freshly baked bread, citrus, nuts, and earthiness from start to finish. Brewed by Goose Island.

LAGUNITAS LITTLE SUMPIN' SUMPIN' ALE   A marriage of hops and wheat in this smooth, hoppy, easy-drinking offering from the Lagunitas Brewing Company.

THE ATOMIC STRUCTURE OF

American Style Wheat

Widmer Brothers Brewing

Clean

Harpoon Brewery

In 1984, Anchor Brewing Company produced the first beer of this style since Prohibition ended—Anchor Summer Beer.

The typical hops used are American: Cascade, Centennial, or Amarillo.

Three Floyds Brewing Company

Smooth

Aw

Goose Island Beer Co.

Bright

This style doesn't utilize the distinctive yeast strain used in German Weissbier, but uses clean fermenting ale yeast instead.

Anchor Brewing Company

Refreshing

Lagunitas Brewing Company

Crisp

This Americanized version of German Weissbier first became popular in the Pacific Northwest of the United States.

Food Pairing

| Salads | Mexican food | Thai food | Light seafood |

Rye Beer

Origin: United States
Color: 3–6 SRM
ABV: 4–9%
IBU: 15–30
Glassware: pint

With influences from ancient rye beer styles, U.S. brewers have used the spicy grain to develop an original and distinct category of beer.

MEETING THE CHALLENGE

When faced with a challenge in brewing, rather than shirking from it, brewers tend to revel in it. Malted rye presents just such a challenge. During the brewing process rye, which has no husk, can cause the mash to become sticky and gummy. Brewers—in particular U.S. brewers—have taken to this specialty grain and utilized its strengths to produce a distinctive product. As rye may be added to a variety of base recipes, the color can range from light golden to a chestnut, with varying colored heads, all generally dense and creamy. The distinctive feature is the slight tang that provides a crisp and refreshing quality. Some examples can be quite hoppy, most have a nice malty center and a refreshing, often sharp, finish.

Three Beers to Try

RED'S RYE PA Caramel, toast, and spicy rye dominate a malty first impression from this beer by Founders. The hops ease in, a bright, piney bitterness, and linger through the finish.

RYE-ON-RYE At 12% ABV, this beer from Boulevard tips the alcohol scale for the style. Citrus hops balance the spicy, malty, and rye body. Whiskey-barrel aging lends notes of wood and complex fruits.

CANE AND EBEL An amber rye, this brew is superbly balanced and drinkable, alternating between citrus, sweet malt, and the tang of spicy rye. By Two Brothers.

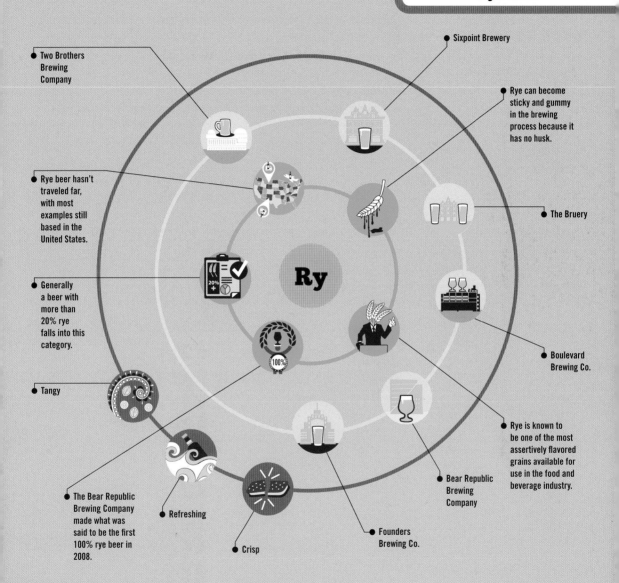

- Sixpoint Brewery
- Two Brothers Brewing Company
- Rye can become sticky and gummy in the brewing process because it has no husk.
- Rye beer hasn't traveled far, with most examples still based in the United States.
- The Bruery

Ry

- Generally a beer with more than 20% rye falls into this category.
- Boulevard Brewing Co.
- Tangy
- Rye is known to be one of the most assertively flavored grains available for use in the food and beverage industry.
- The Bear Republic Brewing Company made what was said to be the first 100% rye beer in 2008.
- Refreshing
- Bear Republic Brewing Company
- Crisp
- Founders Brewing Co.

Food Pairing

| Jerk chicken | Spicy Thai food | Burgers | Roasted pork |

American Pale Ale

Origin: United States
Color: 5–14 SRM
ABV: 4.5–6.2%
IBU: 30–45
Glassware: pint, mug

A brash, bold, yet refreshing style. Americans took the English pale ale and created a brew that is entirely their own.

AN AMERICAN STAPLE

In 1980, Sierra Nevada Brewing Company created the pale ale, upon whose shoulders would stand every American pale ale to come. Giving rise to a craft beer renaissance, this style has become a staple in almost every American brewery's arsenal. Pouring from a deep golden to a near-copper and bursting with hops, there can be notes of oranges, grapefruit, lemon, pine, and grass, some with a bitterness that stretches from first sip to last swallow. There is a definite and firm malt backbone showing some caramel, which supports the hops with a solid balance. Overall, it is a refreshing beer, bursting with flavor.

Three Beers to Try

SIERRA NEVADA PALE ALE The classic continues to impress. Smooth with a hoppy blend of citrus fruit, pine, and floral notes.

BURNING RIVER In this pale ale from Great Lakes, bitter Cascade hops—punching pine and citrus—rest on a foundation of sweet malts and hints of caramel.

MIRROR POND PALE ALE A well-crafted blend from Deschutes in which an inviting nose of bread and citric hoppiness evokes interest and continues on through a clean, crisp body.

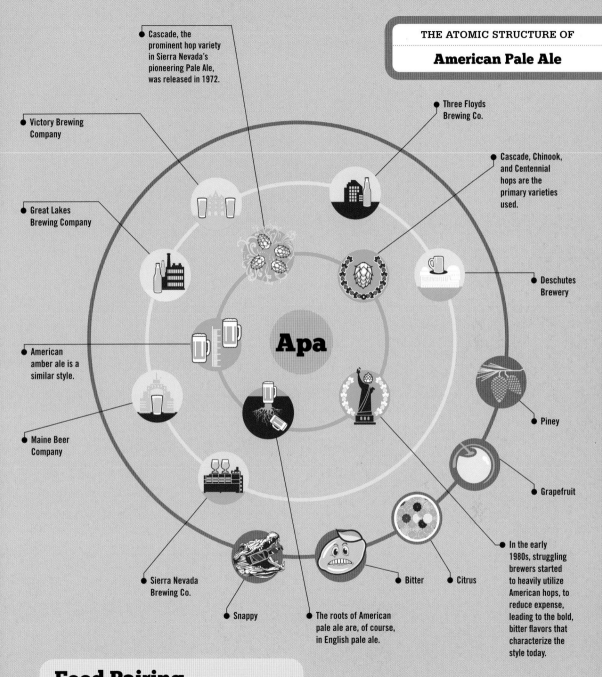

Cascade, the prominent hop variety in Sierra Nevada's pioneering Pale Ale, was released in 1972.

Victory Brewing Company

Three Floyds Brewing Co.

Great Lakes Brewing Company

Cascade, Chinook, and Centennial hops are the primary varieties used.

Apa

Deschutes Brewery

American amber ale is a similar style.

Maine Beer Company

Piney

Grapefruit

Sierra Nevada Brewing Co.

Bitter

Citrus

In the early 1980s, struggling brewers started to heavily utilize American hops, to reduce expense, leading to the bold, bitter flavors that characterize the style today.

Snappy

The roots of American pale ale are, of course, in English pale ale.

Food Pairing

| Citrus salads | Thai food | Burgers | Spicy crab cakes | Mexican food |

American IPA

Origin: United States
Color: 6-15 SRM
ABV: 5.5-7.5%
IBU: 40-70
Glassware: pint, IPA glass

With roots deep in the English IPA style, America's belle of the beer ball is more brash and bitter than its ancestor, and embodies the new craft beer culture.

UNBALANCED AND ASSERTIVE

Today, the American craft beer scene has been overrun with India pale ales (IPAs). And what a good problem to have. Brewers are rising to the competition, making some bitterly assaulting, assertive brews.

In this style "unbalanced" becomes an asset, where the bitterness can be enjoyably abrasive. In color it is deep gold to a ruby-bronze, typically topped with a frothy head. The resinous, citric, floral, piney hops burst on the bouquet. Hop forward on the palate, the aromas also meld on the tongue, balancing on a supportive malty backbone. The flash of malt in the center moves quickly to a dry and often long and bitter finish.

Three Beers to Try

TWO HEARTED ALE A beautifully balanced brew by Bell's, it relies solely on Centennial hops for its citrus and pine notes. Enough malt to make the bitterness pleasantly drinkable.

STONE IPA A smooth mouthfeel softens an intensity of bitterness. Enough malt presence, but piney, spicy, bitter hops are the main event.

60 MINUTE IPA Continuous hopping during the 60-minute boil gives this bitter beauty its name. Pine and citrus flavors are up front, but there is a sweet maltiness behind. By Dogfish Head Brewery.

Beer drinkers who love styles full of hops are called "hop heads."

Ballast Point Brewing Company

Stone Brewing Co.

In the United States, National IPA Day is celebrated in early August.

Dogfish Head Brewery

Bell's Brewery

In simple terms, an IPA is a stronger, hoppier version of a pale ale.

Russian River Brewing Company

IPA has been further broken down into other sub-categories, including East Coast and West Coast IPAs.

Founders Brewing Co.

Resinous

Piney

Grapefruit

Anchor Brewing Company lays claim to brewing the first modern American IPA with their Liberty Ale in 1975.

Citrus

Bitter

Ai

Food Pairing

Spicy Thai food	Indian curries	Jerk dishes	Carrot cake

Wet Hop

Origin: United States
Color: Varies
ABV: 5–7%
IBU: 35–70
Glassware: pint

A well-hopped addition to the American autumn beer lineup, these beers take advantage of the hop harvest and give the brew an extra fresh, hoppy boost.

FRESH FROM THE FIELD

The typical wet-hop beer is founded on a base of pale ale then amped up with fresh-from-the-field hops, often shipped overnight in order to be in the brewer's kettle within 24 hours of harvest. Instead of undergoing the typical drying process, the hops are thrown immediately into the wort, resulting in a fresh, hop-forward brew. While the specific results vary according to the underlying style, wet-hop beers typically have notes of pine, grapefruit, orange, and earth. There is a succulent freshness on both the nose and the mouthfeel. The body can be deep golden to amber, and is topped with a dense, creamy head. Malt is in balance but takes a backseat, allowing the hops to showcase.

Three Beers to Try

NORTHERN HEMISPHERE HARVEST
A wet-hop classic from Sierra Nevada, this beer has a bouquet of orange, grapefruit, and pine, and a bitterness that lasts to the finish.

FRESH HOP   A lemongrass nose melts into a bitter, citrus center on the palate of this wet-hop pale ale from Great Divide. Well-balanced malt and a solid mouthfeel.

HOP TRIP   Notes of juicy citrus and earthy hops are well-balanced by sweet malts in this pale ale. Bitterness lingers through the

THE ATOMIC STRUCTURE OF
Wet Hop

Also called "fresh hop."

Founders Brewing Co.

The term "wet" comes from the fact that the hops have not been dried, but are put in the beer immediately after harvest.

Three Floyds Brewing Company

Earthy

Rogue Brewery

Great Divide Brewing Co.

Piney

Wh

Floral

Deschutes Brewery

Herbal

Sierra Nevada Brewing Co.

The first American-bred hop variety was Cascade, in 1972.

The Sierra Nevada Brewing Company introduced the first American wet-hop beer, Harvest Ale, in 1996.

Grapefruit

Citrus

Food Pairing

| Indian curries | Thai food | Cheddar cheese | Manchego cheese |

Single Hop IPA

Origin: United States
Color: 6-15 SRM
ABV: 5.5-7.5%
IBU: 40-70
Glassware: pint, mug

Single hop IPAs are not so much a strict categorization, but rather an interesting variation on a much-loved brewing style.

RESPONDING TO CRISIS

With the meteoric rise in popularity of IPA (page 32), brewers have crafted myriad imaginative examples of the style, and many different sub-styles have been created in the process. As hop growers continue to create new and hybrid varieties of hops, brewers have sought to produce single-hop beers, isolating and highlighting a specific hop variety.

Accelerating the development of this sub-style was the "hop crisis" of 2007 and 2008, during which a shortage of hops drastically increased costs. This prompted further experimentation in the U.S. brewhouses, and single-hop brews were a product of the trials.

Three Beers to Try

MIKKELLER SERIES This innovative Denmark-based brewery has a revolving single-hop series, in which each beer has an IBU of 100.

SIXPOINT SPICE OF LIFE SERIES
This series focuses on 12 hop varieties, one released each month, the base recipe and process are unaltered, only the hop strain changes.

ZOMBIE DUST Using only Yakima Valley-grown Citra hops, this pale ale—brewed by Three Floyds—is bursting with grapefruit

THE ATOMIC STRUCTURE OF

Single Hop IPA

- Three Floyds Brewing Company
- The Boston Beer Company
- Single-hop beers allow the brewer to focus specifically on characteristics present in only one variety of hops.
- Earthy
- Sixpoint Brewery
- The scientific name for hops is *Humulus Lupulus*.
- Piney
- In order to isolate the hop flavor, many brewers use the same base recipe, changing only the hop variety.
- Floral
- Flying Dog Brewery
- Grapefruit
- Mikkeller
- Some beers not marketed as "single hop" may also utilize just one hop variety. Examples include Bell's Two Hearted Ale and Deschutes Mirror Pond Pale Ale.
- Hops grow upward on bines, in a clockwise direction.
- Citrus
- Bitter

Si

Food Pairing

| Thai food | Burgers | Mexican food | Indian curries |

American Amber Lager

Origin: United States
Color: 6–14 SRM
ABV: 4.8–5.5%
IBU: 18–30
Glassware: pint, pilsner, mug

With rebellion in their brew kettles, American craft brewers of the 1980s set out to brew a lager with character, to provide a response to pilsner's popularity.

AUSTRIAN ANCESTRY

A great big beer basket in which to throw amber-colored American lagers, this category has become a bit of a blanket style. Its foundations lie in Vienna, but the beer has since taken an entirely American path. The malt is more caramelly than bready. The hops are crisply bitter and lean more on typically American pine and citrus notes. Usually light amber to copper in color with an off-white head of varying strength and lacing, the degrees of distinction from Vienna lager vary and what one brewer may call an American amber lager, another may call Vienna lager (page 138).

Three Beers to Try

BROOKLYN LAGER Initial signature American hops of pine and florals ease into a creamy, caramel body that settles in the back of the tongue and finishes dry, with a tinge of bitter.

YUENGLING TRADITIONAL LAGER
From America's oldest brewery comes an iconic brew. It is a bright, clear amber and is smooth, with a sweet grain maltiness and clean hops, with slight notes of citrus.

RIVERWEST STEIN BEER A lasting head tops a creamy, amber base. Smooth on the palate with hop notes of citrus and wood, outweighed by the sweet, caramel center. By Lakefront.

This style has its roots in Vienna lager, a style all but extinct in its country of origin.

Sweet

Clean

Caramelly

Blue Point Brewing Company

Also called American red lager.

A great accompaniment to many foods, this style is a perfect crowd pleaser.

Lakefront Brewery

Malty

Aal

D.G. Yuengling & Son

Creamy

This style was particularly popular in the United States before Prohibition, and would have been much more common than the pale lagers we know today.

Brooklyn Brewery

Shmaltz Brewing Company

Balanced

This style provides a great transition from somewhat flavorless American lagers to higher quality, craft beer.

Capital Brewery Co.

Food Pairing

| Pizza | Grilled meats | Roasted chicken | Aged Gouda | Barbecue |

Double/Imperial IPA

Origin: United States
Color: 8–15 SRM
ABV: 7.5–10%
IBU: 60–120
Glassware: snifter, tulip, oversized wine glass, pint

From the country where more hop varieties are grown than in the rest of the world, comes this hop-heavy style. Big and bitter, with an imperial ABV, it is not for the faint of heart.

HOPS AND MORE HOPS

With the craft beer renaissance in the United States came the love of the IPA. As beer drinkers fell in love with hops, brewers saw room to push the envelope. Enter double IPA.

This style ranges in color from an orange-tinted gold to copper, with a long-lasting, off-white cap of foam. An intensely hoppy bouquet of grapefruit, other citrus, pine, and floral notes burst from the glass. The first sip is hoppy, the aromas melded in a delicious mixture of bitterness. All this adheres to a supportive caramel malt structure, present enough for balance alone. The alcohol is high, but typically well veiled and the finish is long lasting and bitter.

Three Beers to Try

PLINY THE ELDER   One of the greatest examples of the style, this beer from Russian River is assertively hoppy. Bitterness is bold, with grapefruit, grass, and clean pine woven throughout.

HOPSLAM ALE   From Bell's, a stellar Midwest brewer, comes this winter seasonal. Citrus and floral notes erupt on the nose. The palate is introduced with a sweetish caramel that rushes to grapefruit and ends at bitingly bitter hops.

90 MINUTE IPA   Sitting comfortably between 60 and 120 in Dogfish Head's continuously hopped lineup, 90 Minute was the first. The showcase of complex hops is buoyed by a stiff, sweet maltiness.

THE ATOMIC STRUCTURE OF
Double/Imperial IPA

"Breweries are crafting ever-hoppier beers and some are even calling their hoppiest "triple IPAs.""

Bell's Brewery

Stone Brewing Co.

Lagunitas Brewing Company

Double IPAs are best consumed fresh, within a certain period of time often specified by the brewery.

Dogfish Head Brewery

Three Floyds Brewing Co.

Floral

The term "double" in the style name does not denote either double the hops or alcohol.

Piney

Grapefruit

Russian River Brewing Company

The "imperializing" of IPA has led to the same process being followed in various other styles.

Bitter

Citrus

The term "imperial" is borrowed from the Russian imperial stout and denotes a beer with a high alcohol content.

Di

Food Pairing

| Thai food | Cajun food | English cheddar | Triple-cream cheese | Carrot cake |

Pumpkin Ale

Origin: United States
Color: 6-12 SRM
ABV: 5-6%
IBU: 10-15
Glassware: pint

A uniquely American style, pumpkin ale can be spiced like hot cider or as sweet as pumpkin pie.

SEASONAL SPICE

As the leaves start to turn color across the United States, the shelves begin to fill with fall seasonals, one of which is the coveted pumpkin ale.

With gains in popularity, so comes a creativity in brewing and a variety of takes on the style. Pumpkin ale can be light orange to rich copper in color and is typically crowned with a nice tan head. The nose pours out in blends of fresh spices, cinnamon, nutmeg, cloves, allspice, ginger, and, of course, pumpkin. On the palate, there's a blend of the same with additions of caramel and perhaps brown sugar, all layered on a sweet malty backbone. Hops are typically quiet, but provide a bit of balance. A distinctive and delicious treat, to drink more than one is as easy as pie.

Three Beers to Try

PUMKING   Sweet, almost candy-like, this brew by Southern Tier is smooth and viscous. Pumpkin bread notes blend with sweet malt and disguise the 8.5% ABV.

PUNKIN ALE   With origins before its brewery—Dogfish Head—existed, this brew has reason to last. Smooth, sweet, and spicy.

NIGHT OWL PUMPKIN ALE   From Elysian, a brewery with a gambit of the style, comes its standard. Brewed with pumpkin and pumpkin seeds, it is well spiced and deliciously drinkable.

THE ATOMIC STRUCTURE OF
Pumpkin Ale

Some brewers have produced pumpkin stouts.

Coors Brewing Company

Elysian Brewing Company

Southern Tier Brewing Company

Most examples of this style are brewed with pumpkin flesh and/or seeds.

Shipyard Brewing Co.

The flavors in this style can vary widely, from autumn spices to fresh-baked pumpkin pie.

Pu

Pumpkin

Cinnamon

Elysian Brewing Company hosts an annual festival, dedicated entirely to pumpkin ale.

The Saint Louis Brewery

Some early American brewers used pumpkins in place of malt.

Dogfish Head Brewery

Spicy

Food Pairing

| Turkey | Roasted vegetables | Sharp cheddar |

American Amber

Origin: United States
Color: 10-17 SRM
ABV: 4.5-6.2%
IBU: 25-40
Glassware: pint

As with many pale ale styles, the American amber (also called red ale) is a category that is home to—in this case, amber-hued—orphans that simply don't belong anywhere else.

RED AND MALTY

A style category created for darker, reddish pale ales, American amber ale does have a few defining characteristics. Besides its deeper, richer coloring, it has a more malty center than pales, with toasty and caramel notes. The body is richer as well, and the malt moves slightly to the center, sharing the spotlight with the hops. The hops used in this style are typical American varieties and showcase grapefruit, citrus, pine, and flowery notes. It is a balanced, versatile beer with the ability to please a wide variety of palates.

Three Beers to Try

FAT TIRE AMBER ALE From New Belgium, this is the beer that exploded craft beer onto the American market. It is smooth and mild, a great transition into the world of better beer.

NUGGET NECTAR From Tröegs, Pennsylvania, comes a generously hopped amber. The Nugget variety hops lend bitterness while maintaining incredible drinkability.

RUEDRICH'S RED SEAL ALE With a rich maltiness and an abundance of hops, this beer from North Coast Brewing is balanced, flavorful, and smooth. Nice notes of evergreen, citrus, and caramel.

THE ATOMIC STRUCTURE OF

American Amber

Tröegs Brewing Company

Lagunitas Brewing Company

Caramelly

This style has its origins in northern California and the Pacific Northwest.

Flavorful

This style is a member of the pale ale family.

Stone Brewing Co.

Amb

Also called red ale.

Bell's Brewery

Piney

North Coast Brewing Company

New Belgium Brewing Company

Imperial red ale is a newly evolving sub-category of red ale, with higher levels of alcohol and a hoppier bite.

Balanced

American amber is more full, malty, and caramelly than its sister style, American pale ale.

Citrus

Food Pairing

| Burgers | Roasted chicken | Spicy cuisine | Mild cheddar |

American Wild Ale

Origin: United States
Color: 2–26 SRM
ABV: 5.5–10%
IBU: 20–40
Glassware: tulip, goblet, chalice

With a funky, intriguing, and powerful palate, these brews draw a line in the sand. You either love 'em or hate 'em.

A RAINBOW OF COLORS AND FLAVORS

Time to meet another style-bending category. American wild ale is so-called because it utilizes organisms other than *Saccharomyces cerevisiae*, the standard brewing ale yeast, in the brewing process. With the addition of these microorganisms comes an array of flavors, from subtle to brash, resulting in a very distinct and polarizing brew. Colors run the rainbow, from golden to deep garnet to rich, dark brown. The head, too, varies hugely, but is typically fluffy with nice lace. The nose and palate get a medley of funk, from tart and sour to an earthy, barnyard-like mustiness. Most American wild ales are complex and many are quite worth the venture.

Three Beers to Try

SUPPLICATION Russian River, an American pioneer of the style, produces this, a beautiful blend of flavors: tart cherries, must, and fruit. A beer you should try.

LE TERROIR A hazy gold body produces a tart, funky nose. The palate melds sour and barnyard notes in pleasing harmony in this beer from New Belgium.

THE LOST ABBEY CUVEE DE TOMME The base beer, a brown ale, follows the path of barrel aging with cherries and *Brettanomyces* yeast to arrive at a complex wild ale

THE ATOMIC STRUCTURE OF

American Wild Ale

Sour

Musty

Earthy

This style is one of the most inventive in the beer landscape.

Allagash Brewing Company

These beers are often described as "funky," a compliment to their inherent complexity.

Russian River Brewing Company

Complex

Wi

The Lost Abbey (Port Brewing Company)

Brettanomyces is the most commonly employed wild yeast in the United States. *Lactobacillus*, *Pediococcus*, and *Acetobacter* are also used.

Cascade Brewing

New Belgium Brewing Company

Often the necessary wild "bugs" used to achieve the desired flavors come from barrels in which the beer is fermented or aged.

The Bruery

Acidic

Though American wild ale has evolved into a stand-alone style, it has its roots in Belgian brewing.

Food Pairing

| Smoked meats | Creamy or tangy cheese | Salads |

California Common

Origin: United States
Color: 10-14 SRM
ABV: 4.5-5.5%
IBU: 30-45
Glassware: pint

The invention of gold rush-era brewmasters, this style was a refreshing necessity for thirsty, and usually broke, prospectors.

WARM FERMENTATION

During the California gold rush of the 1800s, refrigeration was a luxury unavailable to most. Brewers, forced to be creative, fermented beer in shallow vessels in order to cool it more quickly.

Despite the use of lager yeast, the warmer fermentation temperatures result in some ale-like fruit aromas and flavors in brews of this style. Usually deep gold to deep amber in color, California commons have a rushing carbonation, typical of the first brews of this style ever created. California commons are smooth and brisk, with a medium body. Wood and earthy flavors of hops, as well as bitterness are present, but well-balanced by a juicy maltiness. Today, Anchor Steam Beer is the embodiment of the style, leaving little room for competition.

Three Beers to Try

ANCHOR STEAM BEER The only beer allowed to bear the term "steam," it is a classic. The flavors are a rush, alternating between assertive hops, a malt center, and a long-lasting, bitter finish.

FULLSTEAM SOUTHERN LAGER With its aromatic nose of wood, toast, bread, and caramel, this brew is sessionable, simple, and refreshing.

STEAM ENGINE LAGER Steamworks, a small, Colorado-based brewery produces this classic. Spicy hops blend well with sweet, caramel maltiness.

THE ATOMIC STRUCTURE OF

California Common

Fruity

Caramelly

Toasty

Southern Tier Brewing Company

The term "steam" may have come from the sound of a steam-whistle that was emitted when the keg was tapped, or from the steam coming from the open-air fermenters in which the beer cooled.

This is an exclusively American beer style.

Most of the first breweries to open in California in the mid 1800s brewed this style.

Cc

Woody

Anchor Brewing Company

Anchor Brewing Company has a trademark on the term "steam beer," forcing all others brewed to this style to be called California common.

Refreshing

When Prohibition ended, Anchor was the only brewery, initially, to begin making the style again.

Steamworks Brewing Co.

Fullsteam Brewery

Food Pairing

| Steak | Mexican food | Mellow cheese |

Fruit Beers

Origin: United States
Color: 5–50 SRM
ABV: 2.5–12%
IBU: 5–70
Glassware: pint, oversized wine glass, mug, flute

A category in which creativity blossoms, modern fruit beers have a spectrum of flavors, impacting the taste buds in a powerful way. Typically refreshing, these beers are a perfect summer choice.

A MARKET STALL IN A GLASS

Raspberries, strawberries, cherries, and blueberries. Apricots and apples. Blackcurrant, tangerine, and watermelon. While it sounds like a trip to the farmers' market, it's just another day in the beer aisle. From subtle hints and blends, to bold and bursting palates of fruit, this style can vary in flavor according to the limits of the brewer's imagination. Often intentionally unbalanced, these beers can taste very unlike a beer and can be sweet, fruity, or puckeringly tart. An evolving sub-style, fruit wheat beers are common. The American style wheat lends itself particularly to fruit additions.

Three Beers to Try

RASPBERRY TART From New Glarus, the brewery renowned for this style, comes one bursting with flavor. Ruby with a delicate rose head, it is as advertised: bursting with raspberry and refreshingly tart.

SMASHED BLUEBERRY Coffee, chocolate, and blueberry form an unlikely, but delicious, partnership in this brew. From the Shipyard Brewing Company.

SAMUEL SMITH'S ORGANIC APRICOT ALE Apricot flavors are balanced by a slight tartness and sufficient bready yeast, so you don't forget it's a beer.

THE ATOMIC STRUCTURE OF
Fruit Beers

Magic Hat Brewing Company

Samuel Smith Old Brewery

Portland, Oregon hosts an annual fruit beer festival dedicated to this beer style.

Taste varies by fruit, but should taste distinctively of that fruit.

Abita Brewing Company

Ft

Fruit additions can be either in the form of syrup concentrate or as raw fruit.

Unibroue

New Glarus Wisconsin Belgian Red contains over a pound of cherries in every bottle.

New Glarus Brewing Co.

Lambic and Berliner Weisse styles have added fruit for centuries (page 92 and 76).

Shipyard Brewing Co.

Food Pairing

This beer doesn't have tasting notes—it depends on the fruit used in the brewing.

| Various cheeses | Desserts | |

American Barley Wine

Origin: United States
Color: 10-19 SRM
ABV: 8-12%
IBU: 50-120
Glassware: snifter

In typical American brewer fashion, American barley wine takes the more tempered English version and douses it with hops and greater alcoholic strength.

MALTY SWEET CORE

A bold, strong brew with depth and complexity, American barley wine typically ranges in color from light amber to a deep copper, with some brews being even a bit darker on the scale. Viscous, with a velvet-smooth mouthfeel, it has "legs" that drip from the top of the glass when slowly swirled. Maltiness is at its core, sweetness, caramel, and bread notes are common.

The hop profile has more variety. Some of this style retain just enough bitterness to balance out the tremendous malt forefront, but others have a brash, assertive hop bite, usually in pine and citrus, that carry through to the finish.

Three Beers to Try

BIGFOOT BARLEYWINE STYLE ALE
Rich from first glance to final sip, the flavor medley ranges from a malty nose to an oncoming hop-heavy center, to a lingering and bitter finish in this beer from Sierra Nevada.

THREE FLOYDS BEHEMOTH Big, sweet, and malty, this January seasonal makes the cold winter a bit warmer with an ABV of 10.5%.

OLD RUFFIAN From Great Divide, this barley wine is hugely hopped, but not light on the fruity, caramelly malts either. Creamy and smooth, it is a timeless sipper.

THE ATOMIC STRUCTURE OF
American Barley Wine

Can be a stand-alone dessert beverage.

Bell's Brewery

Great Divide Brewing Co.

Many barley wines increase in complexity after cellaring.

Many beers in this style are aged in barrels after brewing to further their complexity.

Victory Brewing Company

Malty

Usb

Viscous

Stone Brewing Co.

Smooth

Barley wine is so-named due to both its high alcoholic strength and its wine-like complexity.

Sierra Nevada Brewing Co.

Three Floyds Brewing Company

Complex

It is typically hoppier and stronger than English barley wines.

Bitter

Food Pairing

| Hearty foods | Stilton cheese | Bread pudding | Crème brûlée |

American Strong Ale

Origin: United States
Color: 15–35 SRM
ABV: 7.5–13%
IBU: 45–80
Glassware: snifter

A close relative of English old ale, across the Atlantic the style is given a typical American twist of a heftier hop bill.

BIG BEER, HIGH ALCOHOL

This category is a slippery one: vague in specifics, but with a few common threads. American strong ale has become a catch-all category for those dark, viscous, boozy misfits that don't belong anywhere else. Typically it is dark brown to almost black in color, often with ruby highlights. Most examples have a chewy, caramel-sweet malt center, balanced by hops but without overly bitter notes. However, some hugely hopped imperial IPAs have somehow landed in this bucket as well. Essentially, a big beer with high alcohol is about as pinned-down as this style comes. Prepare for a complex, boozy brew.

Three Beers to Try

ARROGANT BASTARD ALE Brewed by Stone, this is an oddly perfected balance of sweet, caramel maltiness and brash, bold hops.

BROWN SHUGGA What was almost a ruined batch of Lagunitas Olde GnarlyWine has become a seasonal favorite. Copious amounts of brown sugar make this a sweet, malty treat.

ROGUE XS DEAD GUY From a base of Rogue's Maibock, this amped-up, hopped-up copper brew envelopes the palate with creamy caramel and sweet breadiness, blended with citrus and

THE ATOMIC STRUCTURE OF
American Strong Ale

Asa

Hair of the Dog Brewing Company

Firestone Walker Brewing Company

American strong ale can be a delicious after-dinner drink.

Boozy

Stone Brewing Co.

These beers are often barrel aged.

Malty

Due to its high alcohol content, this style can typically withstand periods of cellaring.

Rogue Brewery

Many American strong ales are available only as "special releases."

Each year Boulder, Colorado, hosts Strong Ale Fest, where only beers with 8% ABV or more may enter.

Complex

Lagunitas Brewing Company

Bold

The Lost Abbey (Port Brewing Company)

Food Pairing

| Meat stew | Strong cheese | Desserts |

American Brown Ale

Origin: United States
Color: 18-35 SRM
ABV: 4.3-6.2%
IBU: 20-40
Glassware: pint

Based on the more conservative English rendition of the style, United States brewers have amped up the classic, to create a style that is distinctly American.

SWEET AND NUTTY

Despite the robust step up from English browns, the American version maintains the soft, sweet, nutty character that makes the style so inviting. It ranges in color, but is most comfortable as a dark russet graced with a thin beige head. Immediately the aroma tells a tale of big malt and hop bills; sweet notes of chocolate, nuts, and caramel mingle with the scent of fresh, citrus hops. The palate reveals an equally appealing combination of flavors, at times adding cocoa and coffee, and bitterness becomes a significant part of the equation. Balancing itself between English brown ale and light porter, American brown ale justifies its own perfectly delicious niche.

Three Beers to Try

BROOKLYN BROWN ALE Claiming to be a blend of northern and southern English brown styles, this brew is a smooth and drinkable mosaic, with complexities of fruit, chocolate, caramel, and coffee. All washing down with a lingering, clean bitterness.

INDIAN BROWN ALE Big on hops and alcohol, this offering from Dogfish Head still achieves a balance with caramel notes and floral hoppiness.

BENDER Smooth and complex, this brown ale toes the line of sweet and bitter with notes of vanilla and chocolate balanced by a bitter hop bite. From Surly Brewing.

THE ATOMIC STRUCTURE OF
American Brown Ale

Uses exclusively American hops.

Caramelly

Chocolaty

Big Sky Brewing Co.

One of the first, and arguably the most prominent of the style was Pete's Wicked Ale, by Pete's Brewing Company.

Nutty

Smuttynose Brewing Co.

Malty

Aba

Many beer experts and chefs rate this style as one of the best partners to a variety of foods.

Surly Brewing Co.

Rich

This style was dramatically popularized by home brewers in the 1980s.

Brooklyn Brewery

Dogfish Head Brewery

Lost Coast Brewery

When it was first introduced, some called this style Texas brown ale.

Food Pairing

| Burgers | Steak | Manchego cheese | Barbecue | Cajun food |

American Porter

Origin: United States
Color: 22-35 SRM
ABV: 4.8-6.5%
IBU: 25-50
Glassware: pint, nonic pint

Its origins are in the slightly more basic English porter, but with American inventiveness, this style has evolved to house a wide array of distinctive flavors.

AROMATIC AND VERSATILE

Balancing somewhere between medium brown and almost black, many American porters push the envelope in every direction. While most often rich with aromas of roastiness, caramel, coffee and chocolate, some may even possess a shocking hop bouquet. In typical American style, brewers have embraced this style as an essentially blank canvas, and have painted it with everything from bitter hops, to sweet vanilla, or campfire-like smoke. The best versions have a medium-full mouthfeel and a complex flavor profile.

Three Beers to Try

GREAT LAKES EDMUND FITZGERALD PORTER Very deep brown, nearing on black, with a cap of tan foam. Chocolate, coffee, roasted malts and floral hops blend into a beautifully big and bitter end.

FOUNDERS PORTER Lusciously creamy, a blend of dark, roasted coffee and chocolate create a balance with hop bitterness.

ALASKAN SMOKED PORTER Brewed just once each year, this exclusive beer—credited with sparking the smoked beer phenomenon in the U.S.—is worth the wait. The sweet smokiness is not overwhelming and perfectly suited to the style.

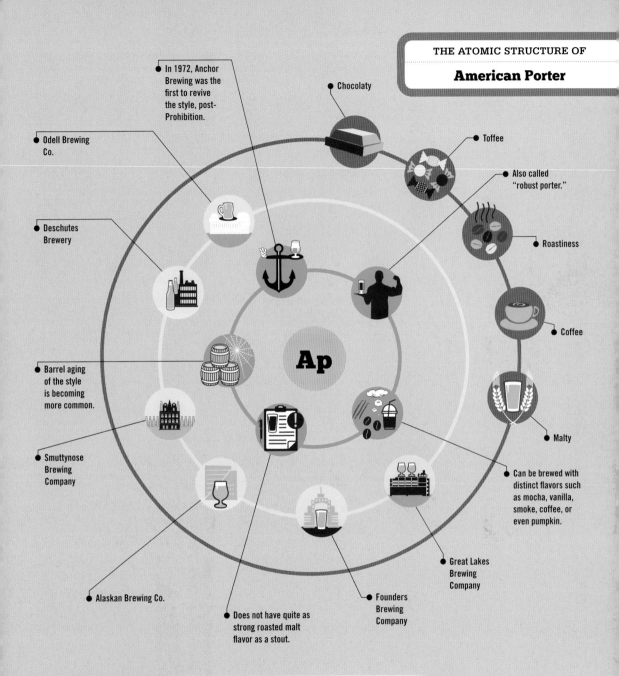

THE ATOMIC STRUCTURE OF

American Porter

In 1972, Anchor Brewing was the first to revive the style, post-Prohibition.

Chocolaty

Odell Brewing Co.

Toffee

Also called "robust porter."

Deschutes Brewery

Roastiness

Coffee

Barrel aging of the style is becoming more common.

Ap

Malty

Smuttynose Brewing Company

Can be brewed with distinct flavors such as mocha, vanilla, smoke, coffee, or even pumpkin.

Great Lakes Brewing Company

Alaskan Brewing Co.

Does not have quite as strong roasted malt flavor as a stout.

Founders Brewing Company

Food Pairing

| Barbecue | Grilled meats | Gruyère cheese | Cheesecake |

Black IPA

Origin: **United States**
Color: **25–35+ SRM**
ABV: **6–9%**
IBU: **50–80**
Glassware: **pint**

A newly coined category, this innovative, seemingly contradictory creation has created a rapidly filling bandwagon of enthusiasts.

DARK ROASTINESS

Black and bitter, this style demonstrates the creativity and willingness to invent in the U.S. brewing community.

The American palate has always loved big, robust flavor profiles, on either end of the hop-malt spectrum. This style combines dark roastiness and chocolate with the notorious resinous, citrus hops of the Pacific Northwest, and produces a pleasingly competing battle of flavors: bitterness, orange, and pine blend with layers of chocolate, roastiness, coffee, and even black licorice. Black IPA has proved a surprising success—yet another beer-making risk that was well worth taking.

Three Beers to Try

SUBLIMELY SELF-RIGHTEOUS ALE
Brewed by Stone in 2007 as a one-off, it soon became available all year round. Opaque black, with huge hops from the nose to the finish.

INIQUITY By Southern Tier, this beer is a shocking contrast of dark color and light body. The huge pine and citrus reveal its style status. The brew's big 9% ABV is well hidden.

WOOKEY JACK Bitter citrus notes on the forefront of this ale from Firestone Walker lean back through the center as a spicy rye emerges. Balanced and quite drinkable.

THE ATOMIC STRUCTURE OF
Black IPA

Bi

- May be reminiscent of the hoppy English porters of the 1800s.
- Deschutes Brewery
- Chocolaty
- Also called "American black ale," "Cascadian dark ale," and "dark IPA."
- Firestone Walker Brewing Company
- Coffee
- Southern Tier Brewing Company
- Roasty
- Freshness is especially important with this style, as the black malts begin to dominate the flavor profile with time.
- Uinta Brewing Co.
- Hill Farmstead Brewery
- The modern version of the style was perhaps originated by Rogue Ales' brewer John Maier, when he tweaked his Brutal Bitter, making it dark in color and with notes of roast and chocolate in 2003.
- Stone Brewing Co.
- Citrus
- Some critics argue that the characteristics of this style are not sufficiently distinct to warrant a separate category.
- Bitter

Food Pairing

| Ribs | Cajun food | Barbecue |

Barrel-aged Beers

Origin: United States
Color: 10–50 SRM
ABV: 5–15%
IBU: 40–100
Glassware: snifter, tulip

Not every beer aged in a barrel has a place in this category, but the explosion of interest in the craft beer sector in this method of brewing justifies the differentiation of this style.

BARRELS OF FLAVOR

Barrel aging is an increasingly widespread method of production, resulting in some complex and inventive brews. The basic concept is simple: A base beer is brewed, typically all the way through fermentation, then moved to wooden barrels for a period of aging. From appearance to aroma and flavor profile, the character of the final beer stems from two main sources: the style of the base beer and the barrel in which it was aged. Base styles can be lagers or ales, light or dark, hoppy or malty. Generally, however, dark, rich, strong beers are best suited to barrel aging. The barrels, most often made of oak, provide hints of the previous resident and can alter the base beer in amazing ways.

Three Beers to Try

BOURBON COUNTY STOUT   One of the first in American craft brewing to experiment with barrel aging, Goose Island produces this barrel-aged Russian imperial stout, with its intense mix of charred oak, chocolate, vanilla, caramel, and smoke.

BEATIFICATION   Famous for its use of wild yeast strains, Russian River has crafted a solid lineup of barrel-aged brews, including this golden offering aged in oak wine barrels.

LA ROJA   Brewed by Jolly Pumpkin in the traditions of a Flanders ale (page 106), this American wild ale is aged in oak barrels and pours a hazy, red-brown. Well-balanced, its flavors move

THE ATOMIC STRUCTURE OF

Barrel-aged Beers

Allagash
Brewing
Company

Firestone Walker
Brewing Company

Bourbon barrels,
by U.S. law, may
only be used once
for bourbon, so
are then often sold
to breweries for
aging.

Jolly Pumpkin
Artisan Ales

Bg

Many barrel-
aged beers,
served in a
snifter, are
the perfect
alternative
to an after-
dinner spirit.

Mikkeller

Wooden barrels were
the most common
way of transporting
beer until they were
replaced by stainless
steel versions in the
1950s.

Russian River
Brewing
Company

Goose Island
Beer Co.

The barrel imparts various
flavors specific to the previous
product aged in the barrel,
from bourbon, whiskey, and
wine to port, sherry, and even
tequila.

This entry doesn't include food pairings or tasting notes, as these depend on the beer's
base style. Try looking up the style of your barrel-aged beer for food pairing suggestions.

Imperial and Hyper Beers

Origin: United States
Color: 8–55 SRM
ABV: 7–40%
IBU: 30–100
Glassware: varies (imperial); snifter (hyper)

With big flavor profiles and characteristic levels of alcohol, these beers start strong and can even approach extreme.

EXTREME BEER

In the modern craft beer world, many have come to think that bigger means better. Imperial Russian stouts (page 66) and imperial IPAs (page 186) have garnered almost cult-like followings. With this desire for bigger and bolder beers, brewers have decided to dabble, bolstering other styles such as brown ales, porters, bocks, and even pilsners to create "imperial" versions. Imperializing typically means that the beer has a substantially greater amount of malt, hops, and higher alcohol content. When done well these beers can be a bolder, more complex version of the base beer. When a brewer takes imperializing to the next level, a hyper beer is created. Hyper beers have an ABV of over 14 percent and can occasionally reach a spirit-like 40 percent.

Three Beers to Try

SHIPWRECK PORTER   Complex, rich, and silky smooth, many stouts don't approach this depth of color, character, and body. This brew from Arcadia has an ABV of 12%.

120 MINUTE IPA   The label evokes images of a hop bomb, yet the end product is sweet, fruity, and smooth, hiding the 18% ABV surprisingly well. By Dogfish Head.

TACTICAL NUCLEAR PENGUIN   BrewDog uses freezing to concentrate their base beer, Paradox, and increase the ABV of this incredibly alcoholic brew to 32%.

Hyper brews are an ideal apéritif. Both imperial and hyper make for a perfect after-dinner drink.

The Boston Beer Company

Boozy

Hyper beers often resemble a spirit more than a beer.

Spirituous

Warming

The Bruery

I

BrewDog

Intense

In 2010 BrewDog released 12 bottles of a brew named The End of History. The bottles for each beer were made out of taxidermied roadkill.

Dogfish Head Brewery

Arcadia Brewing Company

Complex

Samuel Adams Utopias often sells for over $150 for a 24-ounce bottle, and at 27% ABV, it was once the strongest beer in the world. It is presented in a ceramic bottle shaped like a copper-finished brewing kettle.

Hair of the Dog Brewing Company

 Not usually consumed with food.

American Stout

Origin: United States
Color: 30–40 SRM
ABV: 5–12%
IBU: 35–75
Glassware: snifter, pint

The American response to English brews is generally straightforward: make it strong and make it hoppy. In the stout family, U.S. brewers have taken a slightly different path.

A DEPTH OF CREATIVITY

This brew may look very much the same as its English cousin—dark as night, thick, rich, and viscous—but the palate often shows a stark contrast, separating it into a category of its own. Creativity abounds in this style, with not only more hops, but strong additions of espresso, chocolate, vanilla, coffee, raspberry, and cherry. A recent trend receiving resounding applause is the process of barrel aging, which draws out notes of bourbon, rum, and whisky (see also page 208). These nuances have made the brew unique, intriguing, and often boldly different. The popular double stout is not fully double the strength, but has been "imperialized" to add greater depth, flavor, and a higher ABV (see page 210 for other imperialized beers).

Three Beers to Try

SIERRA NEVADA STOUT This stout hits all the high points. It is smooth and rich, delicately balancing a full hop bitterness with robust malt. A classic.

FOUNDERS BREAKFAST STOUT Brewed with Sumatra and Kona blends of coffee, it is smooth and rich. Roasty notes blend with dark chocolate, and the finish is a lingering, bitter delight.

ROGUE CHOCOLATE STOUT The center of this brew is velvety smooth with strong chocolate flavors easing to a balanced bittersweet finish.

THE ATOMIC STRUCTURE OF

American Stout

American double (imperial) stouts age well.

Dogfish Head Brewery

Great Divide Brewing Co.

A brewery will often create several variations of their base stout.

Rich

Sierra Nevada Brewing Co.

Smooth

Robust

Chocolaty

American double stout (also called American imperial stout) is a version of this style with greater alcoholic strength.

Coffee

Bell's Brewery

Rogue Brewery

Many American double (imperial) stouts are so sought-after that brewers have a release day devoted solely to that beer.

Founders Brewing Co.

Barrel aging is common, coaxing out more nuances and complexities than in the unaged version.

Ast

Food Pairing

| Rich meat dishes | Triple-cream cheese | Mellow cheddar cheese | Chocolate desserts | Crème brûlée |

Index of Beers

Index of Beers ... continued

Index of Breweries

Index of Breweries ... continued

General Index

Index of Food Pairing